John J. ó Ríordáin, C.SS.R.

Irish Catholics

Tradition and Transition

Veritas Publications Dublin

First published 1980 by
Veritas Publications,
7 & 8 Lower Abbey Street,
Dublin 1.

Cover design by Bill Bolger

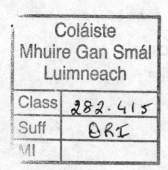
ISBN 0 905092 62 7
Cat. No. 3402

Origination by Healyset, Dublin 2.
Printed and bound in the Republic of Ireland
by Cahill Printers Limited, Dublin 3.

To those
whose memory of a sunset
does not diminish
appreciation of a new dawn.

ACKNOWLEDGEMENTS

The Author and the Publisher are grateful to the following for permission to reproduce copyright material quoted in this work:

Alice Rynne for excerpts from *The Irish Story*;
Allen Figgis & Co. Ltd and Brendan Kenneally for quotations from *A Drinking Cup* by Brendan Kenneally;
Geoffrey Chapman Ltd, a division of Cassell Ltd, for quotations from *The Changing Face of Catholic Ireland* by Desmond Fennell;
Gill and Macmillan Ltd for excerpts from *Old Ireland* by R. McNally, SJ, *Bards of the Gael and Gall* by G. Sigerson, *A History of Irish Catholicism* ed. by Mons. P. J. Corish, *The Life and Writings of St Patrick* by J. Healy, *Irish Spirituality* by D. Ó Laoghaire, SJ, *The Hidden Ireland* by Daniel Corkery, *Studies in Pastoral Liturgy* by T. de Bhál, and *It all happened* by S. Fenton;
Irish Messenger Publications, 37 Lower Leeson Street, Dublin 2, for excerpts from *Our Mass our Life* by Diarmuid Ó Laoghaire, SJ, and *Paidreacha na nDaoine* by S. Ní Dheisighe;
Martin Brian & O'Keeffe Ltd, publishers, and Mrs Katherine B. Kavanagh for quotations from *Collected Poems* by Patrick Kavanagh;
Martin Secker & Warburg Ltd, London, and Stein & Day, New York, for a quotation from *Background Music* by Christy Brown;
Oxford University Press for quotations from *The Irish Tradition* by Robin Flower, *Early English Lyrics* ed. by Gerard Murphy, and *Lives of the Saints from the Book of Lismore* ed. and translated by W. Stokes;
Routledge & Kegan Paul Ltd for excerpts from *Early Irish Literature* by G. Murphy and E. Knott, and *Carolan* by D. O'Sullivan;
St Jarlath's College, Tuam, and Rev. M. Walsh for a quotation from *Knock: The Shrine of the Pilgrim People of God* by Rev. M. Walsh;
Studies, Dublin, for quotations from *Studies*, No. 66, 1928;
The Catholic Truth Society, London, for an excerpt from *Addict for Christ* by F. Johnston;
The Devin Adair Company, 143 Sound Beach Ave., Old Greenwich, Conn. 06870, U.S.A., proprietor, for extracts from *The Story of the Irish Race* by Seamus MacManus;
The Dublin Institute for Advanced Studies for excerpts from *Irish Bardic Poetry* by O. J. Bergin;
The Furrow for excerpts from "Atheism Irish Style" by M. P. Gallagher, SJ, in *The Furrow*, Vol. 25, 1974;
The Mercier Press for quotations from *Early Irish Society* by Myles Dillon, *Irish Classical Poetry* by E. Knott, *The Farm by Lough Gur* by Mary Carbery, and *The Course of Irish History*;
The Royal Irish Academy for quotations from *Ériu*.
While every effort has been made in relation to this work to contact and obtain permission from owners of copyright if any involuntary infringement of copyright has occurred sincere apologies are offered and the owner of such copyright is requested to contact the Publisher.

Contents

Contents

Foreword

Though the general Irish tradition interested me since boyhood, it was not, however, until reading for a masters degree at Seattle University that I decided to investigate the tradition of Irish spirituality in particular. In pursuing the topic I seek to capture the ethos and thrust of Catholic Christianity in Ireland from its inception in the fourth or early fifth century. The text itself was prepared with a North American readership in mind — hence, the inclusion of a certain amount of historical material which may seem commonplace at home.

The analysis presented in Chapter One refers specifically to the Irish scene today but has universal and perennial application to the tensions arising out of the life-giving and death-dealing properties of the institutional Church.

Chapter Two presents the grounding and dynamism of early Irish spirituality. Chapters Three and Four show the continuity and survival of the main characteristics through the vicissitudes of turbulent ages. Chapter Five looks in some detail at the dramatic and traumatic nineteenth-century changes in the Irish Church which revolutionised and in many ways vandalised the Irish traditional approach to God. A final chapter points to the survival of certain key attitudes and elements which, in my opinion at least, call for a very great deal of attention from the post-Vatican II Catholic Church in Ireland.

My thanks are due to Dr Anthony Padovano of Morris Plains, New Jersey, not only for his preface to this work but for reading the original on behalf of Seattle University and indeed for being the very inspiration of the undertaking in the first place; Dr Tom Francoeur of McGill University, Montreal — an official reader of the work, but more importantly a friend and counsellor; Dr Leo Stanford of Seattle and Mrs Helen Wasserlein of San Francisco for their encouragement especially in the early stages of the work.

On the European front, I wish to express appreciation and thanks to An tAthair Seán P. Ó Ríordáin, C.SS.R., Academia Alfonsiana, Rome; An tAthair Diarmuid Ó Laoghaire, S.J., Gonzaga College, Dublin; Siobhán Ní Chléirigh, Baile Móir, Fionn Trá; An tSiúr Aingeal Ní Bhuigléir, Limerick; my parents, family and neighbours in and about Kiskeam, Co. Cork, whose fidelity to the Irish tradition has been an inspiration to me; and, finally, that host of Irish men and women, who, without cost or compliment gave so very generously of their time and

talent — living witnesses to one of the deepest elements in our Christian
heritage.

John J. ó Ríordáin, C.SS.R.
Mount St Alphonsus,
Limerick,
January 1980.

Preface

Spirituality has something to do with how a person or a culture is identified in a profound manner. Spirituality is the concrete way we express the values we believe. It means that we go from doctrine, which is cerebral, to discipline, which is incarnational. Indeed, the manner in which a person actually lives is an unfailing barometer of what he or she truly believes.

It happens frequently that the relationship of spirituality to culture is easily overlooked. Values, discipline, life-style are influenced by the culture in which we mature. Spirituality, therefore, will always be alien unless it is attuned to the culture of the believer. Indeed, the spirituality will be less indigenously vital to the person who pursues it if he or she does not receive it in an idiom or a cultural expression which is familiar, warm, and personal.

Father John J. ó Ríordáin has written a book which seeks out the sources and traces the historical development of Irish spirituality. His study is interdisciplinary. He is immersed in his topic and draws from poetry, history, and theology with equal ease. One of the strongest features of the book is his concern for the preservation of human and personal values, especially when these are threatened by institutional rigidities of the civil or ecclesiastical type.

Irish spirituality has always been sensitive to nature, a sensitivity which may have helped develop the humour which graces Ireland. Father ó Ríordáin's humour at key points in the book, either by an apt quote from an ancient document or by a judicious comment of his own, refreshes the reader.

In addition to sensitivity to nature, Irish spirituality has been especially alive to the mystic dimensions of life and to the pathos of life's impermanence. If a love of nature supports Irish humour, a capacity for mystery has had much to do with the Irish stress on asceticism, austerity, and pilgrimage. Father ó Ríordáin deals with the reasons for and the manifestations of this phenomenon in one of the strongest sections of his book. It does Ireland honour to have one of its sons give so much care and love to the soul and the spirit of a people that has blessed the world and the Church in a remarkable manner.

Irish culture is also famed for its eloquence. At two points in his book, Father ó Ríordáin reminds us of the force of the artistic principle of the "half-said thing". It is this capacity for restraint, for the use of language charged with meaning but not with excess which makes Irish prose and poetry, indeed Irish humour, so delightful. "Delight" is a word which captures well the Irish experience and, in a special way, the charm of this book.

Father ó Ríordáin manages to keep the book from dullness or heaviness even though it traces Irish life from its Celtic origins through its Norman influence to the Reformation and into the contemporary age. He has some very helpful comments on the character and quality of the Irish preference for Rome over the Reformers. The ground, the air, the climate, the sky of Ireland are so Roman Catholic that even Ireland's enemies doubt the sincerity of Ireland's sons and daughters when they say that they are opposed to the Church.

A history so rich and varied, so creative and exuberant, has not been served well by the Anglo-Saxon puritanism and the Continental spiritual theology which influenced Ireland excessively in the nineteenth century. As the author observes, one of the least representative of Irish centuries has become in the popular mind a caricature or stereotype of typical Irish Catholic behaviour. The puritanical repression or Continental formalism of the nineteenth century were not developed naturally in Ireland from its own life force but imported, grafted, and never harmoniously assimilated. These foreign elements took hold in Ireland because the nation became insecure about its identity and its role, embarrassed by its own history, impoverished not only economically but in terms of its own tradition.

Father ó Ríordáin seeks to make Ireland conscious of its rich past and its vital, native spirituality. He questions the pressures which made Rome, caught in the fury of the Modernist controversy, undervalue the ethnic strength and resources of the island nation. Vatican II has been a marvel for the Church, not only because it made Ireland free to be Irish again in its spiritual life but also because it gave us writers like Father ó Ríordáin whose devotion to his Church is exceeded only by his love for his people.

Anthony T. Padovano

1 The institution and the people's faith

That the Church in Ireland is living off the "Faith of our Fathers" and on borrowed time is scarcely a matter for debate. The streamlining, organising and general institutionalisation has been so successful in the past hundred years or so that a decline seems almost inevitable since institutionalisation contains the seeds of its own destruction.

The supreme age of institutionalisation in the Church was perhaps from the reign of Pius IX down to that of Pius XII, an era which coincided exactly with the modern streamlining and institutionalisation of the Irish Church. It is typical of this institutional religion that attention is focused on the person in authority: he is seen or proclaimed as the bearer of truth, the guide, the one to be obeyed. Hence, there is very considerable stress on structure, hierarchy, and other expressions of the institution in the presentation of religion.

Such an approach is ultimately to the detriment of genuine religious tradition and the consequences become obvious: a decline in the general popular transmission of the faith and of prayer. It becomes more and more the work of the institution to take responsibility for these things. The priest and the bishop loom large as authority figures and command great loyalty and equally great opposition. But this opposition is not to themselves as persons — there has never been a shortage of that — but opposition to the institution itself. Besides, there is less and less room for the person of genuine tradition who could and did respect the institution, but never identified with it. When there is far more talk about the bishops than about the faith itself and Christ and Mary, it is time for review and reform because the institution has asserted itself over the tradition.

As the Church became more and more institutionalised, the people handed over greater and greater responsibility to the institution. Church ruling replaced in great part the personal and conscience aspects of the faith. In the old traditional faith, there wasn't perhaps a great deal of personal decision, but there was a great deal of social decision — a mode of life and mores worked out by the people against a background of personal faith in Jesus Christ.

But in the long run, institutionalisation devours the very thing on which it depends and feeds, namely, the faith and personal and social commitment expressed by the people. In the final analysis, one is left with big churches, big plans, streamlined organisations, and nobody there. This process has worked itself through on the mainland of Europe — in France, for example, — and we in Ireland are in danger of repeating it.

The level of religious practice in Ireland is high — highest in the world perhaps. A survey conducted in the Republic in 1973-74 yields the following information:

> 97.00% pray each day.
> 91.00% attend Mass at least once a week.
> 65.60% receive Holy Communion at least one a month.
> 46.50% confess once a month or more often.[1]

A tendency towards euphoria will be immediately checked by a glance at some of the details; for example, the contrast between the 41-50 and the 21-25 age brackets: the former having a Mass-attendance figure of 92 per cent and the latter 74 per cent. Other surveys, although less scientific, tend to corroborate a general feeling that things are not as rosy as would appear from such figures as a 91 per cent Mass-attendance each week.

In a tentative analysis of what he calls "atheism Irish style", Fr Michael Paul Gallagher, SJ, notes that the atheism peculiar to Ireland is not based on philosophical grounds but on "a disenchantment with the externals of Church life and practice", an alienation.[2] "By alienation I mean feelings of withdrawal, even of revulsion from something in which one is externally involved. Obviously alienation from externals can lead to the death of the internals, in so far as those internals of faith in Christ were truly alive or mature in the first place."[3] Father Gallagher adds:

> Another comparatively recent phenomenon may be called the religious unbeliever, someone who leaves the Church to pursue new cults often of Eastern origin or who attaches himself to fundamentalist Christian groups; the key factor here lies in an appeal to spiritual aspirations beside which the Church practice of his upbringing seemed dead and superficial. Once again one comes back to an alienation from a seemingly externalist religion as a trait linking several forms of unbelief.[4]

When the institution assumes more responsibility for the handing on of the faith, it relies very largely on the school and the church; parents feel less obligated to instruct their children. Unfortunately, even in schools run by religious, more often than not, catechetics is the Cinderella of education, while in others, religious instruction "seems to have been geared more to correctness of doctrine and conformism of practice than to conversion of life and heart".[5] An extraordinary amount of emphasis is still being placed on attendance at Mass, though in point of fact, there may be little prayerfulness or living faith in the lives of individuals and the manner of Eucharistic celebration anything but nourishing.

After almost sixteen years of experience in the ministry in this country (Ireland), it is my considered view that the great majority of those who have ceased to practise have been alienated from the faith in a rather simple fashion: they erroneously believe that in rejecting an over-institutionalised religion they are in turn being rejected by or rejecting Christ:

> Yet sometimes when the sun comes through a gap
> These men know God the Father in a tree:
> The Holy Spirit is the rising sap,
> And Christ will be the green leaves that will come
> At Easter from the sealed and guarded tomb.[6]

The time has come, then, for a fresh and reflective look at what Vatican II calls the *sensus fidelium,* notably different from the pre-Vatican II theological term *sensus fidei,* with its impersonal connotation. Vatican II tells us exactly where to look for the truth: to the people, the faithful, the true believing people of God as distinct from the super-ficial, the childish, the careless. If the *fideles* reject a liturgical or para-liturgical piety proffered to them by the institution, it is important to ask the right question. And the right question is not "Why do the people reject it?" but "Where did the institution err in its choice of offering?" As long as clergy, hierarchy or theologians are asking "Why do the people reject it?" they are but talking to themselves and arguing with one another and have lost contact with the masses of the people. But it is the *people* who believe, the *people* who transmit the faith, and it is in the whole *people* of God — clergy and laity at once — that the truth resides.

It is unfortunate that since the nineteenth century in Ireland the role of the people in the transmission of the faith has been neglected to a large extent and native expressions of piety have received scant atten-tion or, worse still, were positively downgraded as Rome extended its policy of centralisation and Anglo-Saxon puritanical culture enveloped the whole land. Now, for the first time in generations, the Church in Ireland has a real opportunity of exploring and expressing a genuine tradition of native piety and, in this critical period of history, of building a modern faith on more authentic foundations.

I am keenly aware of the sense of tradition that lies within myself and my people. It is our strength and our weakness: our strength be-cause we are not easily despoiled of a rich tradition; our weakness because of a tendency to become its prisoners. As the poet said:

> Culture is always something that was,
> Something pedants can measure,
> Skull of bard, thigh of chief,
> Depth of dried-up river,
> Shall we be thus forever?
> Shall we be thus forever?[7]

We are torn between two poles of activity: atavistic wallowing and informed creativity; imprisoning and setting free.

In the remaining chapters of this book I strive to highlight — within
a historical context — the characteristics and thrust of Irish spirituality
throughout the centuries, and in the process isolate the constant elements, believing with French anthropologist Marret that "survivals are
no mere wreckage of the past, but are likewise symptomatic of those
tendencies of our common nature which have the best chance of surviving in the long run".[8] These "survivals" or constant elements, as I have
isolated them, include:

1. Little or no distinction between the material and spiritual world
   and an equal feeling of at-homeness with this world and the world
   beyond.

2. A spirituality in harmony with nature, accepting it, in love with it,
   even in its more violent expressions.

3. A natural religious spirit in the people — "among your earthiest
   words the angels stray".[9]

4. Having a low priority on organisational matters — "plans are only
   for people of limited vision".[10]

5. The traditional faith, firmly rooted in the sacred scriptures which
   the people both knew and loved.

6. A great love for and devotion to the person of Christ, especially in
   his passion and the Holy Mass.

7. A corresponding love for Mary, the angels and the saints, but above
   all, for Mary as Theotokos — Mother of God.

8. The quality of "muintearas", an intimacy and directness in prayer to
   God and in the daily life of the Christian community.

9. The combining of a very strong notion of "localness" with a deep
   sense of communion with the Body of Christ at a universal level
   and an all-embracing congregational quality in both liturgical and
   popular prayer.

10. Hospitality as a living expression of the gospel — the guest is none
    other than the living Christ.

11. Penance and self-denial as a means of entering into the death of
    Christ.

12. The pilgrimage phenomenon.

13. A close bond of unity with the dead giving a sense of fidelity to and
    a spirit of continuity with the past.

Against this background, Vatican II's message of freedom and fidelity is music to the ears; for our popular religious tradition is at once faithful to the point of apparent fatalism and fresh, free-flowing, and unpredictable as a mountain stream.

> A fragrant prayer upon the air
>   My child taught me,
> Awaken there, the morn is fair,
>   The birds sing free.
> Now dawns the day, awake and pray
>   And bend the knee,
> The lamb who lay beneath the clay
>   Was slain for thee.[11]

2 "The Celtic Church"

That St Patrick, Apostle of Ireland, was a tremendous missionary, one of the greatest of all time, is a statement which can safely stand without support from learned footnotes or impressive references. And it is a curious thing that his mission method in the fifth century[1] and that advanced by Pope Paul VI in the twentieth,[2] bear a remarkable similarity. What both are saying in effect is this: take the people as you find them. Build on what you have. Disturb and change only where you must. Listen to the people for they have wisdom in abundance. Graft in the message of Christ without destroying the stock because the people need roots.

Patrick's first introduction to Ireland was abrupt and without formality. A victim of an Irish raiding party on one of their sallies into Roman Britain, Patrick was enslaved for six years in his late teens and early twenties. The years of captivity were not without profound benefit. The youth learned the language and ways of his captors. More importantly, he found himself as a person and interiorised the faith.[3]

But what of the island and its people? The island of Ireland lies in the North Atlantic on the fringe of Europe's continental shelf. Covering an area of about 32,000 square miles, or one third the size of the State of Oregon, it has been inhabited for some eight thousand years since mesolithic man came to hunt the giant deer and fish the teeming rivers.[4] Down through the ages, like waves lapping the shore, wandering peoples established themselves on the island. Most notable among them were the Celts. Arriving in the latter half of the first millenium before Christ,[5] they quickly established supremacy. With the newcomers came much of the myth and mystery, enchantment and romance, so often associated with the Irish and charmingly captured in Thomas Darcy McGee's poem "The Celts":

> Long, long ago, beyond the misty space
> Of twice a thousand years;
> In Erin old there dwelt a mighty race
> Taller than Roman spears;
>
> Like oaks and towers they had a giant grace,
> Were fleet as deers,
> With wind and waves they made their 'biding place,
> These western shepherd seers.

> Great were their deeds, their passions and their sports;
> With clay and stone
> They piled on strath and shore those mystic forts,
> Not yet o'erthrown.[6]

Commenting on what we might call the "Celtic Image", a modern Irish Celtic scholar notes that:

> Down the ages there is a remarkable consistency in the comments of foreign observers writing about the Celts. Thus, while the popular notion of them as reflected in modern literature has undoubtedly been coloured by eighteenth and nineteenth century romanticism with its susceptibility to mist, magic and melancholy, it certainly did not originate there. In fact, many of the attributes which it ascribes to the Celts — eloquence, lyric genius, volatile temperament, prodigality, reckless bravery, ebullience, contentiousness, and so on — have a much longer lineage, appearing in the accounts by classical authors of two thousand years ago.[7]

By the time of Patrick's coming, Ireland had become a thoroughly Celtic land with a rich culture, satisfactory political and legal systems, and a body of religious beliefs and practices with its druids and their elaborate and fascinating mythology. The Roman Empire had expanded as far as neighbouring Britain but fortunately for Ireland and for all of Europe, the imperial ambitions of Agricola were not realised and Ireland suffered no major intrusion until the coming of the Vikings in the ninth century and the Anglo-Normans in the twelfth.

Consequently, the Irish social order, and the learned system which it maintained, remained immune from violent assault until long after Ireland had become Christian and Irish a written language. This must be accounted one of the causes of the remarkable conservative character of Irish learned tradition.[8] It also accounts for Ireland being the sole representative in literature of that great world outside the classic camp, whose thoughts have perished with their lives.[9] Hence, "Ireland is one of the oldest 'kultur-lander' in Europe, and her early literature, as Kuno Meyer puts it, 'the earliest voice from the dawn of West-European civilisation'."[10]

While paganism put up a stiff fight before its final overthrow, Ireland was alone among all the countries of western Europe whose conversion produced no martyrs. Nevertheless, the missionary work of Patrick, though spectacularly successful, was no picnic. In his owns words, the apostle tells us that he "baptised thousands . . . ordained clerics everywhere . . . gave presents to kings . . . was put in irons . . . lived in daily expectation of murder, treachery or captivity . . . journeyed everywhere in many dangers, even to the farthest regions beyond which there lives nobody", and rejoiced to see "the flock of the Lord in Ireland growing splendidly with the greatest care and the sons and daughters of kings becoming monks and virgins of Christ".[11]

But Patrick was fortunate in more than one respect. The people among whom he laboured were religious by nature. Ernest Renan says that the Celts were endowed with "profound feeling and adorable delicacy" in their religious instincts.[12] And the Scottish collector, Alexander Carmichael, notes: "The people were sympathetic and synthetic, unable to see and careless to know where the secular began and the religious ended — an admirable union of elements in life for those who have lived it so truly and intensely as the Celtic races everywhere have done."[13]

Among these warm-hearted people Patrick lived and moved for thirty years, using all the skills of diplomacy, meeting the right people, observing correct protocol; far from disturbing traditional patterns of devotion, Patrick seems to have christened them, thus giving the people a new vision and a new hope. With boundless energy and Pauline zeal he established throughout the land ecclesiastical *communautés de base* out of which a vigourous Church would shortly flourish. Tradition has it that he cursed and he blessed but his writings show him to be overwhelmingly a man who bestowed God's blessings in abundance.

In his spiritual writings, scant though they be, [14] we have abundant proof of the deep personal spirituality which sustained him — an extraordinary knowledge and prayerful use of the sacred scriptures; a profound appreciation of the presence of God frequently expressed in terms of gratitude; the presence of the saving Christ and the indwelling Spirit; and an incredible capacity for prayer so beautifully illustrated in one of the paragraphs of his *Confession* describing his teen-age days in slavery:

> When I had come to Ireland I tended herds every day and I used to pray many times during the day. More and more my love of God and reverence for him began to increase. My faith grew stronger and my zeal so intense that in the course of a single day I would say as many as a hundred prayers, and almost as many in the night. This I did even when I was in the woods and on the mountains. Even in times of snow or frost or rain I would rise before dawn to pray. I never felt the worse for it; nor was I in any way lazy because, as I now realise, I was full of enthusiasm.[15]

Together with the daily crosses and frustrations of a missioner's life Patrick carried with him all his days scars of loneliness, and feelings of being alienated, plus a deep emotional hurt — a snub or rejection or serious let-down by somebody whom he considered to be a close friend.[16] His single-mindedness is inspiring and his unwillingness to allow anyone to mother him is touchingly human and mildly amusing:

> Although I am unskilled in every way I have tried somehow to avoid

being spoiled by my Christian brothers, and by the nuns and the devout women who used to offer me little presents unasked and would even leave some of their jewellery on the altar. When I insisted on giving them back they were offended. But mine was the long-term view and for that reason I used to take every precaution so that the heathens might not catch me out on any issue concerning myself or the work of my ministry.[17]

Irish Celtic Christianity had a tendency towards monasticism from the beginning. This trend became more pronounced after the saint's death, and within a century new monasteries had ousted many of the older Patrician foundations as the important centres of religion and learning. Ultimately Ireland became unique in western Christendom in having its most important churches ruled by a monastic hierarchy, many of whom were not bishops.[18] In fact a monastic system replaced dioceses altogether.[19]

This extraordinary flowering of monasticism owes its origin to a number of factors, not least among them being:

(a) the tendency in the Irish temperament towards an ascetic way of life;

(b) the strong attractive personalities of the great monastic founders;

(c) the influence of St Ninian's Monastery, "Candida Casa" (The White House) in Scotland;

(d) the emphasis placed on study in monastic life stressed by the Welsh reformers Cadoc and Gildas.[20]

Religious communities of women were less numerous but no less celebrated, and St Brigid's foundation in Kildare was unique in sixth-century Ireland for being a double monastery for both men and women,[21] each group following the same rule and using a common church, with the government of the whole community held jointly by the abbess and the bishop-abbot.[22] Tradition, well-founded it seems, suggests that in both temporal and spiritual matters the good lady held 51 per cent of the shares!

Irish society at the time of Patrick and for centuries to follow was an intimate one, having as it did, a socio-political structure with upwards of one hundred and fifty "tuaths" or statelets for perhaps half a million people.[23] "The term tuath", says Professor O'Curry, "was at the same time genealogical and geographical, having been applied to the people occupying a district which had complete political and legal administration."[24] At the head of each tuath was the local king (rí); above him was the provincial king and finally, at the very top, giving a broadly based unity to the entire island, was the High King (Árd Rí).

The king, whether local, provincial or national, was not the lawgiver.

"Laws were adopted by the people in assembly (oenach), only the free-men having franchise."[25] Irish traditional law, known as "Brehon Law", is "the most archaic system of law and jurisprudence of Western Europe".[26] Neither Roman nor Anglo-Saxon in origin, it had reached "full proportions and maturity about the time that Alfred was reducing to order the scraps of elementary law he found existing among his people".[27] Indeed, the system "had sufficient vitality to remain in full force through all the vicissitudes of the country, even till many ages after the intrusion of the Anglo-Normans, in the twelfth century, — who themselves indeed found it so just and comprehensive that they adopted it in preference to the laws of the countries from which they came".[28]

Pre-Christian education in Ireland was the preserve of the numerous native schools of learning. "The introduction of Christianity, and with it of the classical languages, did not supersede the cultivation of the Gaelic . . . but on the contrary it appears to have encouraged and pro-moted it."[29] Conflict there was between the new Latin and the old Gaelic, but it was not the conflict of the oppressor and the oppressed, for Christianity had come to illuminate rather than supplant.

Thus Christian monasticism with its stress on classical learning flourished side by side with the native schools. Indeed, it is to the ever-lasting credit of the early monks that they were open enough and wise enough not only to tolerate the pagan schools but to incorporate and preserve in writing much of the native lore. The Celtic tradition in Europe is preserved in a large number of texts both of prose and of poetry, of which "the most important and valuable are those from Ireland".[30]

Inevitable early tensions between the school systems soon gave way to a spirit of mutual enrichment, though of course there were always those who were anti-intellectual or anti-classical or both. One ancient Irish quatrain runs thus:

> 'Tis sad to see the sons of learning
> In everlasting Hellfire burning,
> While he who never read a line
> Doth in eternal glory shine.[31]

A later poem, attributed to St Columcille, the darling of native and classical schools alike, bemoans the encroachments of Latin to the detriment of the native learning:

> For every school will soon, I vow,
> Be following Latin learning now;
> Old wisdom now they scorn and song
> And babble Latin all day long.[32]

Christianity fitted in rather well with the social system and the cleric found a social niche for himself among the "aes dana" — the men of special gifts — a highly organised professional class of druids, lawyers, doctors, historians and others. "It is hard to resist the conclusion" writes Myles Dillon, "that the structure of the early Church, with its emphasis on the local monastic community rather than on the diocese, was dictated by the political structure of the country; there would be considerable difficulty in the legal relationships of an ecclesiastical unit larger than a tuath".[33]

Perhaps this modelling of the Church on such a local basis, together with the warm personal attitudes of the Celts, fostered one of the deepest, if not the very deepest, and unique features of Christianity as it came to be developed in Ireland. That feature is "muintearas" (familiarity or community-mindedness). It is a constant in the religious and poetical effusions of the Irish from the beginning.

One of the models for understanding God was that of "rí" (king). But in the tuath, the king was not a remote figure, an inaccessible personage in the mould of a medieval European monarch. The king was local — a neighbour's son, a man of the people. Even the "Árd Rí" (High King) was not really remote. "When God is conceived on such a model", says theologian John Macquarrie, "he cannot become too distant and likewise his creation cannot become so profane and godless as to arouse the aquisitive and aggressive spirit of irresponsible concupiscence."[34] Prayer to God, therefore, was a cry from the heart, a tête-à-tête, rather than stilted eloquence. The Martyrology of Oengus, dating from about A.D. 800, uses no less than six native Irish vocables and one loanword with reference to prayer. Warm, endearing expressions are common and perhaps the most popular name for Christ has always been "Mac Muire" i.e. "Mary's Son" or "Son of Mary". An ancient Irish poem on the life of St Patrick describes the spirit of the saint ultimately passing "into the loving friendship of the Son of Mary".[35]

In the same vein the "Lúireach Phádraig", alias the "Lorica" or "Breastplate" of Patrick, ascribed to the saint though not quite as old perhaps, captures the same intimate presence of the Lord. In part it runs:

> Christ with me,
> Christ before me,
> Christ behind me,
> Christ in me,
> Christ beneath me,
> Christ above me,
> Christ on my right,
> Christ on my left.
> Christ where I lie,

Christ where I sit,
Christ where I arise,
Christ be in the heart of everyone who thinks of me,
Christ be in the mouth of everyone who speaks to me,
Christ be in every eye that sees me,
Christ be in every ear that hears me . . .[36]

Perusal of typical Celtic poems and prayers shows that the "Breast-plate" is not at all unique in its sentiments. "Getting up, kindling the fire, going to work, going to bed, as well as birth, marriage, settling in a new house, death were occasions for recognising the presence of God."[37]

Likewise, the sense of God's immanence in his creation is a marked feature of the spirituality of the Celtic Church. A modern translation of a very ancient poem describes paradise as follows:

Round the Tree of Life the flowers
Are ranged, abundant, even;
Its crest on every side spreads out
On the fields and plains of Heaven.

Glorious flocks of singing birds
Celebrate their truth,
Green abounding branches bear
Choicest leaves and fruit.

The lovely flocks maintain their song
In the changeless weather,
A hundred feathers for every bird,
A hundred tunes for every feather.[38]

A poem ascribed to Abbot Manchin Leith who died in A.D. 665, but probably dating from the ninth century, echoes the sentiments of thousands of Irish monks and anchorites of the Celtic Church era:

I wish, O Son of the living God,
O ancient eternal King,
for a hidden little hut in the wilderness,
that it may be my dwelling.

An all-grey lithe little lark
to be by its side,
a clear pool to wash away sins
through the grace of the Holy Spirit.

Quite near,
a beautiful wood around it on every side,
to nurse many-voiced birds,
hiding it with its shelter.

A southern aspect for warmth,
a little brook across its floor,
a choice land with many gracious gifts
such as be good for every plant.

A few men of sense —
we will tell their number —
humble and obedient,
to pray to the King: . . .

A pleasant church and with the linen altar-cloth,
a dwelling for God from Heaven,
then,
a shining candle above the pure white Scriptures . . .

Raiment and food enough for me
from the King of fair fame,
and I to be sitting for a while
praying God in every place.[39]

The love of nature and the spirit of gentleness was often conveyed with a touch of quaint humour. Mochua, for instance, was an anchorite who lived in the waste, without worldly goods of any kind, save a rooster, a mouse and a fly. And the office of the rooster was to keep the hour of matins for him. As for the mouse it would never suffer him to sleep but five hours, day and night, and if he should like to sleep longer, being weary with vigils and prostrations, the mouse would fall to licking his ear till it woke him. And the fly's office was to walk along each line of his psalter as he read it, and when he was wearied with singing his psalms, the fly would abide there upon the line where he left off until he could return again to the saying of the psalms.

Now it came to pass that these three precious ones died. And upon that Mochua wrote a letter to his "anam-chara" or spiritual director, Columcille in Scotland, sorrowing for the death of his flock. St Columcille replied to him — with tongue-in-cheek no doubt: "My brother", said he, "marvel not that your flock should have died, for misfortune ever waits upon wealth."[40]

Indeed that spirit of utter detachment which Columcille was hinting at was very dear to the monk. He revelled in God's world, savoured it to the full, but always in a spirit of detachment knowing that God alone was the ultimate. Again, using an image from nature, another writer illustrates this spirit in St Brigid who

loved not the world:
She sat the perch of a bird on a cliff.[41]

Speaking of the love of nature among the Celts, Kuno Meyer writes:

In Nature poetry the Gaelic muse may vie with that of any other

nation. Indeed, these poems occupy a unique position in the literature of the world. To seek out and watch and love Nature, in its
tiniest phenomena as in its grandest, was given to no people so early
and so fully as to the Celt. Many hundreds of Gaelic and Welsh poems
testify to this fact. It is a characteristic of these poems that in none
of them do we get an elaborate or sustained description of any scene
or scenery, but rather a succession of pictures and images which the
poet, like an impressionist, calls up before us by light and skilful
touches. Like the Japanese, the Celts were always quick to take an
artistic hint; they avoid the obvious and the commonplace; the half-
said thing to them is dearest.[42]

The love of nature and of animals that marked the accounts of early
Irish saints and hermits "recall the Fioretti; and the spirit of the early
Franciscans was, in a measure, anticipated in Ireland".[43]

The spirit of gentleness and loving compassion spills over very much
into warm homely words and images of Christ and his mother Mary.
A very touching hymn to the infant Jesus is attributed to St Íde, "the
foster-mother of the saints of Ireland", whose most famous disciple,
Brendan, is reputed to have been the discoverer of America. "This is
a most tender and beautiful poem", says Fr Ó Laoghaire, SJ, "rendered
intimate by the use of several diminutives which unfortunately are un-
translatable:

> Little Jesus [Íosagán]
> is nursed by me in my little hermitage.
> Though a cleric should have great wealth,
> all is deceit but little Jesus.
>
> The nursing [fostering] done by me in my house
> is not the nursing of one of low degree.
> Jesus with the people of heaven
> is by my heart every night . . .
>
> The sons of nobles, the sons of kings,
> although they come into my country,
> not from them do I expect profit;
> dearer to me is little Jesus . . ."[44]

Besides a delight in the infancy of Jesus there seems to have been an
intense compassion for Christ and Mary concerning the sufferings they
endured. Blathmac son of Cú Brettan, a monk and poet living about
A.D. 700, in over a thousand lines of poetry eulogises Christ's passion
and that several hundred years before the advent of "Stabat Mater"!
Dedicating the lines to "Mary and her Son",[45] he invites the mother of
God to come and share her grief with him:

> Come to me, loving Mary,
> that I may keen with you your very dear one.
> Alas that your son should go to the cross,
> he was a great diadem, a beautiful hero . . .

> When every outrage was committed against him,
> when capture was completed,
> he took his cross upon his back —
> he did not cease being beaten.

> The King of the seven holy heavens,
> when his heart was pierced,
> wine was spilled upon the pathways,
> the blood of Christ flowing through his gleaming sides . . .

> It would have been fitting for God's elements,
> the beautiful sea,
> the blue heaven, the present earth,
> that they should change their aspect when keening their hero . . .

> The King was patient
> at the crucifixion of his only-begotten,
> for had his good elements known,
> they would have keened sweetly . . . [46]

Blathmac upbraids the Jews for shameless breach of kinship ties in putting Christ to death:

> Of shameless countenance and wolf-like
> were the men who perpetrated that kin-slaying;
> since his mother was one of them
> it was treachery towards a true kinsman. [47]

But if the Jews were harsh towards "Jesus, darling son of the virgin"[48] there was sympathy in abundance for him from other sources:

> Tame beasts, wild beasts, birds
> had compassion on the son of the living God;
> and every beast that the ocean covers —
> they all keened him. [49]

Having keened the passion of Christ, Blathmac, approaching stanza one hundred and fifty and the end of his first poem, petitions Mary:

> Let me have from you my three petitions,
> beautiful Mary, little bright-necked one;
> get them, sun of women,
> from your son who has them in his power . . . [50]

> For you, bright Mary, I shall go as guarantor;
> anyone who shall say the full keen shall have his reward.
> I call you with true words, Mary, beautiful queen,
> that we may hold converse together to pity you heart's darling. [51]

A poem ascribed to St Columcille but probably a tenth-century composition is in the very traditional form of a litany:

Christ's cross over this face, and thus over my ear.
Christ's cross over this eye. Christ's cross over this nose.
Christ's cross over this mouth. Christ's cross over this throat.
Christ's cross over the back of this head. Christ's cross over this side.[52]

The writer goes on to enumerate a variety of other aspects of the human anatomy "from the top of my head to the nail of my foot", as well as asking to have "Christ's cross over my community. Christ's cross over my church."[53]

A blessing before leaving on a journey — an eleventh-century composition perhaps — combines the Trinitarian theme with that of Jesus and Mary:

May this journey be expeditious, may it be a journey of profit in my hands!
Holy Christ against demons, against weapons, against slaughters!

May Jesus and the Father, may the Holy Spirit sanctify us!
May mysterious God that is not hidden in darkness, may the bright King save us!

May the cross of Christ's body and Mary guard us on the road!
May it not be unlucky for us! May it be prosperous, expeditious![54]

This prayer is also in the style of a "Lorica" or "Breastplate". The prayer-form takes its origins from St Paul's image of putting on the spiritual armour of the Lord. It is a sort of litany and a very popular one at that. Another example of the same is that of St Fursa, who went to Gaul in the sixth century and is still honoured at Péronne in Picardy — anciently known as "Perrona Scottorum" (Péronne of the Irish):

> May the yoke of the Law of God be on this shoulder,
> the coming of the Holy Spirit on this head,
> the sign of Christ on this forehead,
> the hearing of the Holy Spirit on these ears,
> the smelling of the Holy Spirit on this nose,
> the vision that the People of Heaven have in these eyes,
> the speech of the People of Heaven in this mouth,
> the work of the Church of God in these hands,
> the good of God and of the neighbour in these feet.
> May God be dwelling in this heart
> and this man belong entirely to God the Father.[55]

Of the "Lorica" type prayers Gougaud says:

> These long enumerations of petitions, these series of adjurations, ardent invocations, these enumerations of spiritual and bodily dan-

gers . . . the whole, divided by pious aspirations pressing effusions towards God and the Saints, strong sentiments of repentance, compunction, of distrust of self, that is what gives to these ancient Celtic prayers an appearance and a very special quality.[56]

The love of Christ naturally led to love for neighbour and this was aided in turn by a tradition of hospitality among the people of the land even before the coming of Christianity. Of Finn McCool, the pre-Christian folk hero, it was written:

> Turn brown leaves to gold
> On an autumn day,
> Turn white waves to silver —
> Finn would give all away.[57]

Of course lack of hospitality carried its own punishment — generally in the form of disastrous reputation and sometimes an early grave. Before Patrick's time, Eochaidh, a prince and hostage, managed to escape from captivity. On being refused hospitality at a house he had to proceed home on an empty stomach. But as soon as he had been adequately refreshed he returned with some followers and proceeded to burn down the house and kill the son of the inhospitable man.[58]

The Irish word for hospitality is "oigedchaire", literally "guest-loving". In the Christian vision of life the guest was always Christ:

> God in Heaven!
> The door of my house will always be
> Open to every traveller.
> May Christ open His to me!
>
> If you have a guest
> And deny him anything in the house,
> It's not the guest you hurt.
> It's Christ you refuse.[59]

From another source we have the following dialogue:

Cuimmine: "And what about the welcome of fire and bed?"
Comghan: "It is the same as journeying to Rome on the way of Paul and Peter."[60]

And again:

> Although fasting and prayer are good,
> Although abstinence and fast are good,
> better is it to bestow a thing
> and keep one's mouth shut.[61]

Even in prayer, any form of inhospitable conduct is reprehensible. A prayer made for oneself alone is known in Irish as a "paidir ghann", literally a "scarce prayer", or "stingy prayer".

This same spirit of generosity to the point of prodigality characterised the peoples' response to the Christian message and must be held responsible in large measure for the incredible response to a total religious commitment on the part of the new Irish Church. Even in Patrick's own lifetime, there was an extraordinary flowering of evangelical and religious life. Recounting the fact in his *Confession,* Patrick says:

> There was, in particular, a virtuous Irish lady of noble birth and great beauty, already grown to womanhood. I had baptised her myself. A few days later she came to us with a problem on her mind. She had been advised, in a divine message, she said, to become a nun and thus to approach more nearly to God. Thanks be to God, six days later she carried out what he had proposed and dedicated herself with a fine enthusiasm to God. So, too, other virgins. Their fathers disapprove of them, so they often suffer persecution and unfair abuse from their parents; yet their number goes on increasing. Indeed, the number of virgins from our converts is beyond counting, and to these must be added the widows and those who forego their marriage rights. Of them all the women who live in slavery suffer the most. They have to endure terror and threats all the time. But the Lord gives grace to many of his handmaids and although they are forbidden, they follow him courageously.[62]

The developing Irish monasticism had its own peculiar flavour. "A sixth-century Irish monastery", writes Tomás Ó Fiaich "must not be pictured like one of the great medieval monasteries on the continent. It was much closer in appearance to the monastic settlements of the Nile valley or the island of Lerins than to later Monte Cassino or Clairvaux. Even the Latin word "monasterium" when borrowed into Irish under the form "munitir" was applied not to the buildings but to the community."[63] Indeed it is only fitting that "muintir" should mean the household rather than the house, for the Celts were ever more interested in people than the institutions in which they dwelt.

As for daily routine in the monastery, St Columbanus, a sixth-century Irish monk and perhaps the greatest European of his day, wraps it all up in one simple sentence: "Pray daily, fast daily, study daily, work daily."[64]

Daily prayer centred on the divine office, with Eucharistic liturgy on Sundays and feasts. There was no uniformity or rigidity in celebrating either — a typically Celtic trait. Variety was not felt to endanger unity even in matters of faith — "sunt autem quidam Catholici" (there are indeed some Catholics) said Columbanus in speaking of those whose mode of celebrating the divine office differed from his.[65] No wonder then that his feelings ran so high when one of the popes of his day attempted to force the Irish Church into line in the famous "Paschal Controversy".[66]

Early Irish literature and manuscript materials abound with references to the divine services, especially the vigils or night office which was so dear to the tradition. The little monastic bell which summoned all to prayer was indeed a sacramental of special worth. An eighth- or early ninth-century liturgical book introduces this marginal quatrain as a grammatical illustration:

> The wind over the Hog's Back moans,
> It takes the trees and lays them low,
> And shivering monks o'er frozen stones
> To the twain hours of nighttime go.[67]

Another monk consoles himself in his choice of a bell over a belle:

> I'd sooner keep my tryst
> With that sweet little bell
> The night of a bad winter mist
> Than risk a ravenous female.[68]

Yet another monk is having problems of concentration and cannot keep his mind on his psalter:

During the psalms they wander on a path that is not right;
they run, they disturb, they misbehave before the eyes of great God.

Through eager assemblies, through companies of foolish women,
through woods, through cities — swifter than the wind . . .

Neither edged weapon nor the sound of whip-blows keeps them down firmly;
they are as slippery as an eel's tail gliding out of my grasp . . .

O beloved truly chaste Christ to whom every eye is clear,
may the grace of the sevenfold Spirit come to keep and check them.[69]

The Stowe Missal — a manuscript written in the monastery at Tallaght, Co. Dublin, in the early seventh century — gives us considerable information on the celebration of the Eucharist. As well as a confession of sins, the recitation of the litany of the saints, and the scripture readings, there were numerous prayers, spontaneous and otherwise; but regarding the general outline "an examination of the different elements . . . shows that its affinities are with the Church in Gaul, but that it has been influenced by the liturgies of Spain, Milan, and (above all) Rome".[70]

At prayer in general, standing was the usual posture adopted, but on solemn feasts the brethren were allowed to sit during part at least of the ceremonies. They showed exceptional zeal in reciting the psalms and other vocal prayers — one Fiacc, having been baptised by Patrick, is reputed to have learned to read the psalter in Latin in a matter of fifteen days.[71] Genuflections and prostrations in phenomenal numbers were the order of the day — and of the night — in Irish ascetical practice. Oengus the Culdee is said to have made three hundred genuflections every night.[72] Though standing throughout the Eucharistic liturgy, the people prostrated themselves on the floor in absolute silence and reverence during the consecration.[73] A third posture at worship, that of kneeling with outstretched arms in the form of a cross, is most colourfully portrayed in the story of St Kevin who is said to have prayed so long with outstretched arms that the birds came and nested in the palms of his hands.

Ascetical practices were very much part of the Irish expression of faith and "it is hard to say whether Irish saints or Indian yogis practised the cruelest austerities".[74] The "Féilire" or martyrology of Oengus the Culdee is an interesting source of information on the various practices. Findchu, for example, used to lie the first night with every corpse that was brought to his church for burial. Scothine expressed his understanding of penance and mortification by sleeping, not with one dead person, but with two live young ladies. As a form of mortification, this latter practice has long since ceased in Ireland. Columcille, who died in A.D. 597, like many another of his saintly contemporaries slept all alone in his bed, but then who would want to share the cold slab of stone on which he rested, and the pillow of like material whereon he laid his head. As for flagellation, the "Féilire" mentions it up to two hundred and eighty times as practised by Oengus himself.[75]

Fasting was a most common form of mortification. "Fast daily", said Columbanus. Indeed, the whole life of the monk was one of total self-denial, while fasting till later afternoon was practised on Wednesdays and Fridays throughout the year except from Easter to Pentecost. Forty days of fast was celebrated not once but three times in the year — the forty days before Easter, another forty before Christmas, and yet another forty ("The Fast of Elias") after Whitsuntide.[76]

Three days of the week in the Irish language take their names from these fasting habits:

Wednesday = "céadaoin", literally "céad aoin", first fast (of the week);
Friday = "aoine" or "an aoine", fast, or the fast, fasting, abstinence;
Thursday = "díardaoin", literally "dia idir dhá aoin", the day between
    the two fasts.

With all the fasting, the paschal season stood out as a time of great joy and relaxation from mortifications. It has been called the "Great Easter" — something comparable to heaven, an incentive to the monks to keep up the struggle and so come to the "land of many melodies, musical, shouting for joy . . . feasting without extinction . . . partaking of the Great Easter".[77]

Fasting "against" somebody as a means of gaining redress, exerting moral pressure, or cursing, was also common in ancient Ireland. There are examples of fasting on the land of the person one wishes to curse;[78] of St Patrick fasting against a slave-owner to gain redress for the oppressed;[79] and fasting even against God himself is not unknown as the following delightful little anecdote from the "Féilire" testifies. The story goes that the abbot of Dairinis once saw a little bird weeping and making great lamentation. "O my God," said the abbot, "what has befallen the creature yonder? Now, I swear that I will not eat anything until the cause be revealed to me." He had not long to fast, for an angel soon not more do men bewail him than the creatures, and among them the you no longer. Molua, Ocha's son, is dead. And for this cause the creatures lament him, for that he never killed any creature little or big. And not more do men bewail him than the creatures, and among them the tiny bird that you see."[80]

Together with his injunction to pray daily and fast daily, Columbanus enjoined on his monks to "study daily, work daily". There was of course the necessary work on the land for material sustenance, but added to that was the great concentration on learning in general and on arts and crafts such as metallurgy, monumental sculpture, and manuscript copying with the host of back-up services which accompanied them. Far from rejecting native pre-Christian art forms, the Celtic Church developed them to such a peak of refinement that survivals like the Book of Kells[81] and the Ardagh Chalice[82] are sources of wonder and overwhelming admiration to the most skilled craftsmen of all ages.

The scholar *par excellence* in Ireland was the scribe, and the dignity and perfection of his art is an indication of the reverence accorded to sacred scripture, which so frequently formed the subject matter for transcription. In the Book of Kells, to which I have already alluded,

> . . . all the well-known patterns of Celtic art appear in the ornamentation: the dots around the capital letters, the interlaced bands, the vine and grape clusters, strutting peacocks, writhing serpents, biting animals — all combine with a lavish use of colour: crimson, blue, gold, green. The text, too, is varied by the use of scarlet and mauve inks.

> The capital letters are lost in such a wealth of decoration that they are no longer legible; their identity is solved by the following script. This obscurity is said to have been deliberate, as a sort of protection against the profane. The capitals, in fact, are used rather like the rood screen before the altar, a kind of symbolic check interposed between the inner mysteries of the place of sacrifice and the multitude without. The capital letters are evidence of the tendency to mystification which is such a well-known trait of the Celtic mind— a tendency indeed omnipresent in the whole mysterious art.[83]

Still treating of the Book of Kells, Alice Curtayne continues:

The Book of Kells poses several questions. Does the prominence given to Our Lady confirm special veneration of her in the early Irish Church? Biblical experts have their own angle on the Book; historians and linguists have others. The de Paors, archaeologists, made a bold jump recently over what would at first sight seem an unbridgeable chasm and pointed out that James Joyce's *Finnegans Wake* finds an antecedent in the Book of Kells. Joyce and the anonymous scribe had at least Celtic mystification in common.[84]

Kells, where the book was compiled, was but one of a host of monastic schools which had sprung up all over the country in the fifth and sixth centuries offering learning to all and sundry — young and old, slave and free, rich and poor, foreigner and native-born. Indeed, there were so many Englishmen at school in Armagh that their part of the campus was known as "The Saxon Third".[85] Clonmacnoise on the River Shannon, founded by St Kieran in A.D. 545, became Ireland's most romantic educational centre. Affectionately known as "Kieran's plain of crosses",[86] it had in its heyday several thousands of home and foreign students. The thirty-three year old founder died within months of establishing Clonmacnoise, but the great university flourished for over a thousand years until its suppression by Henry VIII in the sixteenth century. Some sense of the tradition and continuity and sanctity of this most hallowed site is captured in an old Gaelic poem by the bard O'Gillian, and finely but freely translated by T. W. Rolleston:

> In a quiet watered land, a land of roses,
> Stands St Kieran's city fair;
> And the warriors of Erin in their famous generations
> Slumber there.
>
> There beneath the dewy hillside sleep the noblest
> Of the clan of Conn,
> Each below his stone with name in branching Ogham
> And the sacred knot thereon.
>
> There they laid to rest the seven Kings of Tara,
> There the sons of Cairbre sleep —
> Battle-banners of the Gael, that in Kieran's plain of crosses,
> Now their final hosting keep.
>
> And in Clonmacnoise they laid the men of Teffia,
> And right many a lord of Breagh;
> Deep the sod above Clan Creide and Clan Conaill,
> Kind in hall and fierce in fray.
>
> Many and many a son of Conn, the Hundred-Fighter,
> In the red earth lies at rest;
> Many a blue eye of Clan Colman the turf covers,
> Many a swan-white breast.[87]

These monastic schools, far from decrying classical learning, promoted it vigourously as Arsene Darmesteter attests:

> The classic tradition, to all appearances dead in Europe, burst out into full flower in the Island of Saints, and the Renaissance began in Ireland seven hundred years before it was known in Italy. During three centuries Ireland was the asylum of the higher learning which took sanctuary there from the uncultured states of Europe. At one time Armagh, the religious capital of Christian Ireland, was the metropolis of civilisation.[88]

With the collapse of the Roman Empire and the ensuing Dark Ages, Ireland became a promised land. Bede, the great English historian of the seventh century, speaks of nobility and commoners alike forsaking their native country either for the grace of sacred learning or a more austere life: "And some of them indeed soon dedicated themselves to learning, going about from one master's cell to another. All these the Irish willingly received, and saw to it to supply them with food day by day without cost, and books for their studies, and teaching, free of charge."[89] Of Bede's countrymen, Montalembert pertinently comments: "The Anglo-Saxons, who were afterwards to repay this teaching with ingratitude so cruel, were of all nations the one which derived most profit from it."[90]

Such was Ireland's reputation that when, in neighbouring countries, a man of studious habits was for a time missing from his usual haunts, it was concluded that he had gone to Ireland to seek education.[91] And in the days of Charles the Bald, if anybody on the Continent professed to know Greek, he was deemed to be an Irishman, the pupil of an Irishman or a damn liar.[92]

But the movement of people was not all in the direction of Ireland. Irish missionary endeavour among the peoples of mainland Europe from the sixth to the ninth century was quite phenomenal. "Into the foreign lands these swarms of saints poured as though a flood had risen", wrote St Bernard. "Of these," he said, "one, St Columbanus, came to our Gallic lands and built a monastery at Luxeuil, and was made there a great people. So great a people was it, they say, that, choir following after choir, the divine office went on unceasingly and not a moment of day or night was empty of praise."[93]

Columbanus himself, who died at his monastic foundation in Bobbio, Italy, in A.D. 615, was the most noted example of Irish scholarship in the Europe of his day. "We need only to glance at his writings", says Celtic scholar Jubainville, "to be at once convinced of his wonderful superiority over St Gregory the Great and the Gallo-Roman scholars of his time."[94] This restless, fearless, stormy and sainted intellectual has more than a hundred monasteries directly or indirectly to his credit. Not only was he fearless in the face of the most powerful and wicked civil rulers, but his love for the Holy See did not deter him from, provoked him rather, to rebuke the Pope himself, urging him not to allow "the head of the Church to be turned into its tail . . . for in Ireland it is not a man's position but his principles that count".[95]

The reasons for leaving home and fatherland were varied: a penitential exercise (one imposed by a confessor perhaps), missionary zeal for evangelisation, a search for solitude on the Continent, or a desire to go on pilgrimage to Rome, Jerusalem, Compostella and, later, Irish Continental shrines such as those of Kilian at Würzburg or Fursa at Péronne – the latter having a church dedicated to St Patrick dating from about A.D. 700.[96]

Pilgrimage for religious purposes was undoubtedly the prime motive of those who went abroad in the early days of Irish Christianity. They left their country for Christ's sake as Adamnan says of Columcille: "de Scotia ad Britanniam, pro Christo peregrinari volens, enavigavit" (he set sail from Ireland for Britain desiring to be a pilgrim for Christ).[97] There are three kinds of pilgrimage, says the "Life of Columcille" in the Book of Lismore:

(a) leaving one's country for love of God, and forsaking vice for virtue;

(b) leaving one's country in body and with no change of heart; from this, one derives "neither fruit nor profit to the soul"; it is sheer waste of time and energy;

(c) having the *desire* to go on pilgrimage when the call of duty demands a life on the home front.[98]

Another reason noted by Walahfrid Strabo, the illustrious ninth-century historian and abbot of Reichenau on Lake Constance, is the fact that wandering is second nature to the Irish, "quibus consuetudo peregrinandi iam paene in naturam conversa est" (their habit of going on pilgrimage has now become second nature).[99]

Whatever the motivation or cause, the desire to be "on the move" is incontestably evident, whether over uncharted waters towards Iceland, Greenland or the North American continent, or to somewhat more accessible spots such as Rome, Jerusalem, Compostella di Santiago, or even Kiev – at a time when most human beings were not given to wandering farther than a few leagues from their own front door!

The pilgrimage to Rome was the heart's desire of the Irish religious. St Molua once asked his superior for permission to go to the Eternal City. The abbot had some reservations, but the good St Molua pushed his case with urgency, exclaiming, "Nisi videro Romam cito moriar" (Unless I see Rome I shall not live long).[100] Another monk is not quite so enthusiastic – perhaps he has had personal experience:

> Who to Rome goes
> Much labour, little profit knows;

> For God, on earth though long you've sought him,
> You'll miss at Rome unless you've brought him.[101]

But no matter what the motivation or intention, pilgrimage overseas was not always possible and one had to be content with pilgrimages at home, a devotional practice ever held in high esteem. The abbess of Clonbroney was once approached by a would-be pilgrim: "I desire to go overseas on pilgrimage", said the petitioner. The abbess replied: "Were God to be found overseas, I too would take ship and go. But since God is near to all that call upon him, there is no constraint upon us to seek him overseas. For from every land there is a way to the kingdom of Heaven."[102]

From surviving manuscript material we can get a picture of these *peregrini* who "live for us not merely as historical figures but as actual persons, restless wanderers, shameless beggars, men of deep personal religion, lovers of learning, graceful poets and original thinkers, representatives of a civilisation where the standard of religion and learning was high, in the point of learning distinctly higher than the contemporary continental standard".[103] Of this superior learning the Irish made no secret. The story is told of two Irishmen who came as merchants of wisdom to the court of Charlemagne and there advertised their "merchandise": "Si quis sapientiae cupidus est veniat ad nos et accipiat eam, nam venalis est apud nos" (If anyone is desirous of wisdom let him come to us and buy, for we have it for sale).[104] No one among the Irish, as Gerard Murphy points out, "not even the gentle Sedulius himself", was backward in entitling himself "Sophus", "Sophista", or "Sapiens" ("wise man", "a sophist", "a wise man").[105]

Needless to mention, the *peregrini* displayed on the Continent a variety of characteristics familiar to the culture and tradition of the homeland. Thus, for example, we find them spreading the practice of spiritual direction and frequent confession — the latter hitherto unknown on the Continent. We find too the Celtic warmth and directness in prayer, as illustrated in a little quatrain composed for the safe arrival of one Dermot coming overseas to visit Sedulius. For his safety, Sedulius "the most poetically minded and the most skilful as a craftsman of the poets of his day"[106] prays:

> Christe, tuo clipeo Dermot defende, precamur,
>   Cumque suis sociis veniat hanc laetus in urbem.
> Sis proreta potens nostris in navibus, alme:
>   Te sine, cunctipotens, prospera nulla queunt.

> (Christ, defend Dermot with thy shield, we pray;
> and with his companions may he come in joy to this city.
> Mayest thou be a powerful pilot in our ship, O Beloved One:
> without Thee, O All-powerful, nothing can prosper.)[107]

Another characteristic of the home culture was not lacking either: that of satire. John Erigena, an Irish philosopher in the days of Charles the Bald and the greatest genius at his art of the period between Augustine and Aquinas, having fallen out with his good friend Hincmar of Rheims, satirised him thus:

> Hic iacet Hincmarus cleptes vehementer avarus:
> Hoc solum gessit nobile, quod periit.

> (Here lies Hincmar, a greedy grasping ruffian.
> This one noble act did he do: he died.)[108]

On another occasion when dining with the king of the Franks at a table where wine and wit abounded, Charles the Bald quipped at the expense of the Irishman:

> "Quid distat inter sottum et Scottum?
> (What is there between a sot and a Scot [i.e. an Irishman]?)

The irrepressible Erigena shot back:

> "Tabula tantum".
> (Only the table.)

In its missionary and scholarly endeavour, the Irish Church was not preoccupied with detail in the matter of organised and delineated apostolate. In this lay the strength and weakness of the Irish Church both at home and abroad. It preserved the "human touch", the warmth, the intimacy, the personal, but the price paid was a certain lack of structuring which might have made for greater permanence. It is a typically Celtic trait. Still, of her endeavours at home and abroad, Professor Zimmer, most eminent of Celtic scholars says:

> Ireland can indeed lay claim to a great past; she can not only boast of having been the birthplace and abode of high culture in the fifth and sixth centuries . . . but also of having made strenuous efforts in the seventh and up to the tenth century to spread her learning among the German and Romance peoples, thus forming the actual foundation of our present continental civilisation.[109]

But in its weaker aspect, in that lack of enduring organisations, – if that indeed be weakness – there was, too, a profound aspect of the Celtic spirit, a preoccupation with mystery and the "after life", a sensitivity to the transience of life as experienced, a feeling that things are not what they seem. On this a modern Irish scholar writes:

> In all the vast range of traditional material handled by the monastic scribes and literati nothing seems to have captured their imagination quite so completely as the theme of the voyage to the happy otherworld . . . Françoise Henry in her monumental study of Irish Art

has drawn a sensitive and revealing comparison between the accounts of the voyage to the otherworld and the complex, elusive ornament of Celtic art. She finds both characterised by the same aversion to rigidity and to barren realism and she sees in the illuminated pages of the Gospel books the artistic reflex of the polymorphic otherworld: "This multiform and changing world where nothing is what it appears to be is but the plastic equivalent of that country of all wonders which haunts the mind of the Irish poet, and in which all those impossible fancies seem to come true to which the world does not lend itself."[110]

I have chosen a poem from the eleventh century as a suitable ending to this chapter since that century saw the last stages of the Celtic Church. The author, Máel Ísu Úa Brolchán (d. 1086) fittingly expresses himself in the twin languages of that Church: Gaelic and Latin. It is a song of hope and trust, an earnest cry from the heart for the one thing necessary: love of God. A translation of the original, preserving the metre, has been made by Dr George Sigerson,[111] but first, a stanza of the poem as penned by Úa Brolchán:

> 'Deus meus, adiuva me.
> Tuc dam mo sheirc, a meic mé Dé.
> Tuc dam do sheirc, a meic mo Dé.
> Deus meus, adiuva me.

Sigerson translates as follows:

Deus meus adiuva me (My God, assist Thou me),
Give me Thy love, O Christ, I pray,
Give me Thy love, O Christ, I pray,
Deus meus adiuva me.

In meum cor ut sanum sit (Into my heart that it whole may be),
Pour loving King, Thy love in it,
Pour loving King, Thy love in it,
In meum cor ut sanum sit.

Domine, da quod peto a te (Lord, grant Thou what I ask of Thee),
O, pure bright sun, give, give to-day,
O, pure bright sun, give, give, to-day,
Domine, da quod peto a te.

Hanc spero rem et quaero quam (This thing I hope and seek of Thee),
Thy love to have where'er I am,
Thy love to have where'er I am,
Hanc spero rem et quaero quam.

Tuum amorem sicut vis (Thy love as Thou mayest will),
Give to me swiftly, strongly, this,
Give to me swiftly, strongly, this,
Tuum amorem sicut vis.

Quaero, postulo, peto a te (I seek, I claim, and I ask of Thee),
That I in heaven, dear Christ, may stay,
That I in heaven, dear Christ, may stay,
Quaero, postulo, peto a te.

Domine, Domine, exaudi me (Lord, Lord, hearken to me),
Fill my soul, Lord, with Thy love's ray,
Fill my soul, Lord, with Thy love's ray,
Domine, Domine, exaudi me.

Deus meus adiuva me,
Deus meus adiuva me.

3 The late medieval period

What we normally refer to as the Celtic or pre-Norman Church dates
from the coming of St Patrick in the fifth century to the coming of
the Normans in the twelfth. The sixth to the ninth centuries are commonly designated as "The Golden Age", an age which was harshly, if
gradually, terminated by the Viking raids which bedevilled Irish monasteries from the eighth to the eleventh century. Nevertheless, we find in
the Irish Church at the end of the eleventh and the beginning of the
twelfth century sufficient vitality for a programme of self-reformation
to be initiated. That reform was called for is scarcely to be doubted.
Among other things, deeds of violence were frequent, even against
clergy, religious and Church property in breach of the age-old tradition
recorded in the "Féilire":

> Now these are the four laws of Érin:
> Patrick's law, not to kill the clerics;
> and Adamnan's law, not to kill women;
> Daire's law, not to kill kine;
> and the law of Sunday, not to transgress at all [thereon].[1]

Nevertheless, native learning flourished and the metalwork, archi-
tecture and manuscript illumination of the time demonstrate the assimi-
lation of many Viking, Roman, Gothic, and other foreign elements into
the mainstream of Irish artistry. Demand for manuscripts was great and
the scribe as in days of old applied himself to his skilled and disciplined
task, though day following on day of this absorbing task must have
wearied more than the author who leaves us a little human sidelight on
his life. In translation from the Irish it runs:

> My hand is weary with writing;
> my sharp great point is not thick;
> my slender-beaked pen juts forth a beetle-hued
> draught of bright blue ink.
>
> A steady stream of wisdom springs
> from my well-coloured neat fair hand;
> on the page it pours its draught of ink
> of the green-skinned holly.

> I send my little dripping pen unceasingly
> over an assemblage of books of great beauty,
> to enrich the possessions of men of art —
> whence my hand is weary with writing.[2]

A trend to give the Irish language a more prominent place than that of Latin developed in the tenth and continued through the following centuries, while the effort at replenishing libraries after the Viking destruction made the copying and importation of books a high priority. With a decline in the monastic schools more and more private families took it upon themselves to preserve and pass on to posterity a learned tradition in literature, and sufficient manuscripts have survived from the twelfth and following centuries to testify to an energetic pursuit of poetry, storytelling, law, philosophy and medicine.[3]

Two further subjects dear to this intellectual élite were history and devotional literature. Both of these are of special interest to us in this work.

On the historical scene the twelfth century was a turning point in Ireland. Two primates, first Cellach and then Malachy, both saints, spanned the first half of the century and spearheaded reform. In 1111, a national synod held at Raith Breasail, near Cashel, Co. Tipperary, presided over by the primate and the High King, divided Ireland into episcopal sees which replaced the old monastic organisation, and with few modifications, has survived down to the present day. This was the beginning of a new era given impetus both from the Church in the homeland and the Church on the Continent. The old monasteries and their schools were still in existence but, for the first time in its history, Ireland came to be administered by a diocesan system parallel to that on the mainland of Europe. A Church based solely on the monastic system left much to be desired in the field of pastoral care. More balance between a monastic and a diocesan structure was needed. Cellach initiated this in the first part of the century but died while visiting Munster in 1129. His death, wake and funeral are recorded in the Annals of Loch Cé:

Cellach, comharb of Patrick, i.e. the chief bishop of the West of Europe; a pure, illustrious virgin; the only head whom Foreigners and Gaeidhel (i.e. Irish), both laics and clerics, obeyed; after having, moreover, ordained bishops and priests, and persons of every degree besides; and after having consecrated very many churches and cemeteries; after having bestowed jewels and wealth; and after having imposed faith and good manners on all, both laity and clergy; and after a life of Mass-celebration, fasting, and praying, and after unction and choice penance, resigned his soul into the bosom of angels and archangels, in Árd-Patraic, in Mumha, on the kalends of April, the 2nd (feria), in the twenty-fourth year of his abbotship, and in the fiftieth year of his age. His body was conveyed, truly, on the 3rd of the nones of April, to Lis-mor-Mochuda, according to his own will; and it was waked with psalms, and hymns, and canticles, and was honourably interred in the tomb of the bishops on the day before the nones of April, on the 5th feria.[4]

Cellach's successor, Malachy of Armagh, was a man of the same calibre and pushed ahead with reform. The work begun at Raith Breasail was brought to a successful conclusion at the Synod of Kells in 1152. Though death had come to him shortly before the synod, the success of the assembly was in large measure due to St Malachy.

St Bernard of Clairvaux, personal friend and biographer of Malachy, was given to hyperbole when compiling an inventory of the evils of his day — a fact to be borne in mind when reading his account of Malachy's Ireland:

When he began to administer his office, the man of God [Malachy] understood that he had been sent not to men, but to beasts . . . never had he found men so shameless in their morals, so wild in their rites, so impious in their faith, so barbarous in their laws, so stubborn in discipline, so unclean in their life. They were Christians in name, in fact they were pagans — 'Christiani nomine, re pagani'.[5]

While admitting guilt on many counts, Ireland cannot have been as bad as St Bernard claims since in fact it produced St Malachy himself, whose person, spirit and general disposition so patently captivated the saint of Clairvaux. Bernard, brought up in a tradition of Roman law, was quick to see any other legal system as barbarous, but the Celtic Church in Ireland had shown enough independence of spirit to adopt Christianity without exchanging the Brehon Law for the Roman code.

At any rate, the great St Malachy got to work in traditional Irish style and spent "entire nights in vigil, holding up his hands in prayer",[6] with the result that

Barbarous laws disappeared, Roman laws were introduced: everywhere ecclesiastical customs were received and the contrary rejected: churches were rebuilt and a clergy appointed to them: the sacraments were duly solemnised, and confessions were made: the people came to church, and those who were living in concubinage were united in lawful wedlock. In short all things were so changed that the word of the Lord may to-day be applied to this people: Qui ante non populus meus nunc populus meus (those who before were not my people are now my people).[7]

One of the elements of friction during the work of reform was the tension which existed between the Irish Church in general and the newly-established Hiberno-Norse sees which gave allegiance to Canterbury. During the Viking period the Norse gained a foothold on the coast and established a number of towns and trading ports. Chief among these were Dublin, Waterford, and Limerick. In time the Norse became firmly established in the Christian faith, but their culture was not Gaelic and their connections were with foreign parts, England in particular, rather than with the island on which they lived. Malchus, the first Bishop of Waterford (1096-1135), was a monk of Winchester. It is not certain when Donatus was consecrated first Bishop of Dublin, but it is probable that it took place about 1028 when Sitrick, the Norse king of Dublin, went to Rome on pilgrimage and contributed to the collection of "Peter's pence". Where and by whom Donatus was consecrated we do not know, but we do know that his successor, Patrick, was consecrated at Canterbury, and that Malchus of Waterford was consecrated by St Anselm in Canterbury. Both Anselm and his predecessor, Lanfranc, laid claim to primacy of Ireland but as the reform progressed the problems were gradually resolved, and the connection between the Norse-Irish and Canterbury was quietly buried in 1140.

Gilbert, the Norse Bishop of Limerick, was not consecrated at Canterbury and played a very vital role in the twelfth-century reform. As papal legate he presided over the Synod of Raith Breasail and introduced into Irish ecclesiastical affairs some of the much needed Norse organisational ability — with admirable results it must be added.

The other key event which makes the twelfth century memorable in the annals of Ireland is the Norman invasion of 1169. These Norman-French knights had neither literary nor scholarly interests. War and conquest, military advancement and social organisation were their priorities. Within a century two-thirds of the country was in their hands, but by then they had reached their zenith and were already on the run before the recovering Gaelic nobility. Nevertheless, a host of Norman-French names were to become part of the Irish scene; and Gaelic culture, manners, law, dress and speech were to be adopted by such prominent invading families as the FitzGeralds of Kildare and Desmond, the Butlers of Ormond and the de Burgos of Connaught. So thoroughly did they adopt Irish life-style that they were said to be "Hibernicis ipsis Hiberniores" (more Irish than the Irish themselves),[8] but, as historian John Ryan, SJ, very rightly points out, "this claim was exaggerated because the Norman lords did not renounce their emotional attachment to the English Crown".[9] Such an attachment was meaningless to a native Irishman.Thus a cleavage remained.

The wars, feuds, squabbles and multiplicity of assassinations perpetrated by Norman on Norman, and on Norman by native Irish and vice versa were a matter for bitter lamentation by Irish annalists during the two centuries which followed the invasion. Little wonder too, that one Richard Wye, Bishop of Cloyne, Co. Cork, took unliturgical advantage of a requiem Mass which he was celebrating in Dublin Castle on the occasion of the death of Phillipa, Countess of March, in 1381, and "did after beginning the accustomed preface introduce these words":

Eterne Deus,
duo sunt in Momonia
qui destruunt nos et bona nostra,
videlicet comes Ermonie
et comes Dessemonie
cum eorum sequacibus,
quos in fine destruet Dominus
per Christum Dominum nostrum.
Amen.

(Eternal God,
there are two in Munster
who destroy us and what is ours.
These are the Earl of Ormond
and the Earl of Desmond
with those who follow them,
whom in the end the Lord will destroy
through Christ, our Lord.
Amen.)[10]

The bishop was proceeded against for slander, schism, and heresy and deprived of his see, but anybody who reads the history of the times may well be forgiven for siding with this man who "with high voice said and sang these damnable words".[11]

In the continuing unrest caused by the Normans, the Irish Church suffered most perhaps. For one thing, the old monastic school system had broken down and no modern university on the lines of Paris or Oxford had arisen to replace them. To say that the Irish were without high education would be untrue, but it was haphazard, fragmented, and ineffectual. Furthermore, the new religious orders — Franciscans, Dominicans, Cistercians, Augustinians and others — were in a state of continual turmoil due to racial strife.

Through Malachy's personal friendship with St Bernard, the Cistercians were introduced into Ireland in 1142. The Benedictines had established themselves some years earlier and many more emerging Continental orders were soon to follow while the Canons Regular of St Augustine supplanted many of the ancient Irish monastic foundations. The invading Normans brought with them several English and Continental monks, thus establishing rival monasteries of the same orders, or attempting to impose foreign superiors and abbots on communities of Irish monks. This extension of the conquest to monastic precincts led to continual apartheid, gerrymander, and political jockeying, which more than once erupted in bloodshed amounting to massacre. At the 1291 Franciscan chapter in Cork, for example, the sons of the gentle St Francis decided that action speaks louder than words, so that at the end of one plenary session the chapter-hall was strewn with the dead bodies of sixteen delegates. "The enmity grew so fierce that in the early four-teenth century one Brother Simon declared solemnly that it was not a sin to kill an Irishman and, if he himself did such a deed, he would not on that account refrain from celebrating Mass."[12]

In an atmosphere of such acrimony, there was little likelihood of genuine progress. How an Ireland without an invader might have de-veloped medieval schools of philosophy, theology, and spirituality is for ever a matter of conjecture.

But the great codices and lesser manuscripts which were written in Irish and have survived the ravages of the centuries have much to tell us about the life, spirit, and spirituality of the people between the twelfth and the sixteenth century. Again and again we find old themes recurring, old attitudes surviving: pilgrimage, asceticism, fasting, alms-giving, hospitality, the passion of Christ, devotion to Mary and the saints (native and foreign) and, of course, the after-life. All these and more besides were part and parcel of the furniture of Irish Christianity.

Pilgrimage of all kinds was common — to holy wells, monastic shrines, churches. One of the fringe benefits to stem from the existence of the Norse towns was an improvement in shipping facilities, and a con-sequent increase in the number of foreign pilgrimages — to Rome, Jerusalem, Compostella or other Continental shrines. Needless to say, jubilee years in Rome drew exceptionally large numbers of pilgrims from Ireland. The pilgrimage to the island of Iona off the western coast of Scotland, for ever associated with the beloved Columcille, retained its popularity as a place of pilgrimage in medieval times. At home, many places throughout the land are mentioned by the annalists and other sources as popular places of pilgrimage for the purposes of prayer and repentance: Clonmacnoise, Glendalough, Croagh Patrick Mountain, St Patricks's Purgatory and a host of other lesser centres throughout the length and breadth of the country.

Perhaps at this point it might be well to single out for more detailed treatment the most famous of all pilgrim sites in Ireland, that of St Patrick's Purgatory. The fame and fortune of the pilgrimage is of con-siderable interest. Situated on a tiny lake-island in Co. Donegal, the "Purgatory" has been associated with St Patrick from time immemorial. Though challenged from time to time, there is no real evidence to dis-pute the authenticity of the tradition that the saint did spend some time in prayer and penance in that vicinity or on the island itself. Before his coming, the spot may well have been the site of a pagan shrine, as tradition asserts the presence of an extraordinary, monstrous, and ex-tremely ill-behaved serpent in the lake. The tale giving the aetiology of Lough Derg — the name of the lake — tells how it was called Finnlough (the fair lake) until Patrick, having prayed and cast his crozier at the ser-pent, so wounded it that the profusion of blood turned the lake red.

Thus the saint decreed that the fair lake be known thence till Judgement Day as Lough Derg (red lake).

The earliest written material we have on the subject comes to us from Henry of Saltrey, an English Benedictine from Huntingdonshire, who, around 1152, wrote a treatise "De Purgatorio S. Patricii". According to Henry's informant, a soldier who made the pilgrimage, the most traumatic aspect of it was making one's way through a cave on the island. The cave itself is the real "Purgatory" where St Patrick prayed and did penance, and in it the pilgrim is expected to encounter a motley variety of other-world personalities from all known centres of population in that land of mystery. For this reason, people were not recommended to enter the cave at all but, if they insisted, the machinery for proceeding was well defined:

> It was necessary in the first place to get the permission of the bishop by letter addressed to the Prior [of the community who served the place of pilgrimage] and the bishop always dissuaded the pilgrim from attempting it. Having presented the bishop's letter to the Prior, the latter also dissuaded the adventurous individual, but if he persisted in his purpose, he had to remain five days in retreat; then a Requiem Mass was celebrated, at which he received the Holy Communion, and he finally made his will. After these somewhat terrifying preliminaries, if he was still determined to visit the cavern, the clergy, in solemn procession, accompanied him to the pit's mouth, singing the litanies, the Prior unlocked the door, the adventurer took holy water, signed himself with the sign of the Cross, and entered the cave, which was closed after him. Next day the clergy went again to the pit's mouth; if there was no appearance of the pilgrim, he was given up for lost, but if he did appear, he was taken out, the clergy with great joy conducted him to the church, where he spent fifteen days more in thanksgiving for his deliverance, which was almost regarded as a mark of predestination.[13]

So famous was the pilgrimage on the Continent that illustrious personages flocked to it from all over Europe — Hungary, Italy, Rhodes, Spain, France, the Netherlands, England — and three metrical versions of Henry of Saltrey's story were published in the thirteenth century, followed by one in the fourteenth and another in the fifteenth. The thirteenth-century set was published in French, the other two in English.

A cool and clinical Dutchman visited the shrine in the fifteenth century. Not realising that there might be some truth in the remark that the Irish are a "natio poetarum fabulis facilis credere" (a nation of poets prone to believe in fables),[14] and on being asked for some contribution of a financial nature, he made haste to Rome and informed Pope Alexander VI that the whole business was a fraud. Alexander duly issued a brief ordering the suppression of the pilgrimage and the destruction of the cave "quia fuit occasio turpis avaritiae" (because it was an occasion of base avarice).[15] His orders were carried out on St Patrick's day, 17 March 1497. If the truth were told, far from ordering its destruction, the same Alexander Borgia might well have derived a considerable and much needed spiritual uplift from a trip to the renowned penitential station.

Happily, and to the surprise of nobody, the pilgrimage soon revived and a new "cave" or "prison" was constructed on a neighbouring island. Peter Lombard (c. 1620) describes it as "a narrow building roofed with stone which could contain twelve, or at most fourteen, persons kneeling two-and-two. There was a small window, near which those were placed who were bound to read the Breviary".[16] Tadhg Dall Ó hUiginn, the sixteenth-century Gaelic poet, refers to the "cave" as "a haven to cleanse the soul from torment, bright Rome of the west of the world".[17] Tadhg Dall, who probably went on pilgrimage himself, speaks of the healing properties associated with the Lough Derg pilgrimage:

> Without, on the far side of the cave, is a pool to wash all from their wounds, a shining smooth-banked lake-spring.
>
> No wound, however grievous, was ever dipped 'neath the wide, spreading pool, the bright-pooled, dry, clear, warm, stream that it would not bring out of it hail.[18]

Henry of Saltrey's informant describes in some detail his guided tour of the world beyond, thus drawing upon himself and his story the scorn of the Dutchman. His story nonetheless struck a very homely note with the Irish who felt as much at ease in the other world as in this. In fact, a special category of Irish folk-tales entitled "echtrae" (adventure) have as their chief motif the other world, known variously as "The Promised Land", "The Land of the Living", "The Delightful Plain", "The Many-coloured Land", and "The Land of the Young" (Tír na nÓg) — this last ascription being perhaps the most popular of all. In the words of Myles Dillon:

> Here is introduced most strongly the Celtic magic, the imaginative quality for which Irish literature is well known . . . The Irish Other World is a country where there is neither sickness nor age nor death; where happiness lasts forever and there is no satiety; where food and drink do not diminish when consumed; where to wish for something is to possess it; where a hundred years is as one day. It is the Elysium, the Island of the Hesperides of the Greeks; the Odains-Akr, the Jörd Lifanda Manna, of the Norse. Alfred Nutt pointed out that it finds its closest analogues in early Greek mythology, and he suggests that it represents ancient Indo-European tradition.[19]

In the late medieval period, the old love of nature continued to assert itself. Agallamh na Seanórach (The Colloquy of the Ancients), a twelfth-century work purporting to be a dialogue between St Patrick and a pre-Christian folk-hero named Caílte, demonstrates the survival of the nature-loving spirit — with an injection of Judaeo-Christian culture, as witnessed in the use of the term "thrice fifty". The expression "thrice fifty" of course crept into Gaelic culture and language from the number of psalms. Describing the Scottish island of Arran, that ever-popular hunting resort of the ancient Irish, Caílte says: "Thrice fifty flocks of birds frequented it, of every colour, blue and green and grey and yellow." And again: "Sweeter it was than any music to hear the cry of the birds there, as they rose from the waves and coasts of the island."[20]

The person of Christ, particularly in his passion and cross, was still very central to Irish spirituality in the medieval period, as was expression of devotion and love for his mother Mary. It is not easy to separate mother and son.

Christ's crucifixion for our sake is spoken of in terms borrowed from the Brehon Laws as the payment of the "eric" or blood-fine. The poems of the thirteenth-century author Donnchadh Mór Ó Dálaigh include two very interesting works on the cross in which the medieval legends of its origin from the Tree of Paradise are used. "These are fine poems in their way," comments Eleanor Knott, "not unfit to be compared in some measure with some of the well-known Latin pieces on the same theme."[21] Knott goes on to quote a translation (from the Irish) of the opening verses of one:

A beacon to the world is the holy Cross,
conspicuous tree of fair brown surfaces;
roads that are the brightest to look on
are the seals of this tree of the five wounds.
The cross of Jesus, relic which gives succour to all;
many are the kinds in which the golden-comely bright dry supple one
from the fair seed of the wood of paradise is called a beacon . . .
From its side came the light that dispersed the darkness of this world;
it is not a beacon unworthy of trust,
that which drowned [i.e. expunged] the Lord's original claim [i.e. freed repentant man from the consequences of the Fall].[22]

An Anglo-Norman of the fifteenth century, one Richard Butler, in testing his skill at Gaelic metre, did not master the technicalities with great accuracy, but he does capture something more valuable: the sincerity and spontaneity of a traditional Irish prayer:

Rí an Domhnaig mo dhochtúir-si
is Muire liaigh dom leighis
's a chroch neamh gan rothuirsi
go sgaraid mhé rem theinnis.

(May the King of the Sunday, my doctor,
And Mary, my physician in my illness —
And the holy Cross — grant, that without too great sorrow
I shall be parted from my illness.)[23]

Donnchadh Mór Ó Dálaigh (d. 1224), one of the most outstanding
poets of the age having written many poems of a more or less secular
nature, thinks it fitting to pay a tithe on his talent. Taking up a theme
dear to many a Gaelic poet and through an application of Brehon Law,
rather than the Pauline theology of the Mystical Body, he claims brother-
hood with Christ:

Tabhradh Mac ar seathar sinn
ar chionn eaga go hinill
rath críche gion go ndligh dhámh
ar na ciche or ibh th'adhbhar.

Dlighidh an Coimdhe rom chum
trocuire d'fhéachain oram
's é 'na dhearbhrathair 'n-a dhiaidh
deagh-mháthair Dé 'n-a deirbhshiair.

(May the son of you, my sister,
Bring me safely through life —
Though I do not deserve a good end —
You from whose breast He drank your substance.

The Lord who formed me
Must look mercifully on me;
After all, He is my brother
Since I have the good mother of God for a sister.)[24]

Yet another poet, this time a sixteenth-century one who is living in
exile in Scotland, sings the praises of Mary and appeals for her protec-
tion especially at the Judgement, an event which, in Irish tradition, is
due to take place on a Monday:

As I dread that on the Monday of the Tribute — a hard case — the Red
    Cross
and the death of Jesus will confront me, beguile thy Child on that day.[25]

Though the theology of the poet sounds strange to us today, it was typical among the poets of the time and presumably among the preachers.[26]
In the same poem, the author adds a lovely human touch when he
grieves with Mary in her sorry lot as her son is in the tomb:

The Virgin Mary suffered as much as the Passion . . .
while God's Son was in the grave after it,
and her cheeks red as embers.[27]

Titles of honour and comments on her physical beauty abound through the rest of the poem: "O harp of tuneful strings", "O cheek of the hue of the berry", "O smiling face", "O protecting shield", "O mighty soil of virtue", etc..[28] Such title-giving was normal practice among Gaelic writers of all ages.

The aforementioned Tadhg Dall Ó hUiginn speaks tenderly of Mary too:

> A Mhuire ínghean Mhaoil Mhuire
> gur chuireas ort m'ionghuire,
> beag nar cailleadh, a chiabh lag,
> gach daingean riamh dá ránag.
>
> (O Mary, daughter of "Maol Mhuire",
> until I entrusted to you my shepherding,
> almost every fastness which I reached was forced,
> thou lady of clinging tresses.)[29]

And again:

> Máire ínghean Mhaoil Mhuire
> gnúis ríoghdha, rún gheanmnuidhe;
> bean ós mhnáibh braonbhrogha Breagh,
> aonrogha cháigh dá chineadh.
>
> (Mary, daughter of "Maol Mhuire".
> regal in aspect, chaste in mind;
> a woman excelling those of Bregia's dewy castle,
> the favourite of all her kindred.)[30]

Though the medieval period abounds with songs and prayers about Jesus and his mother and the passion, I can only be selective here. As a final example the following extract from a mystical poem of the period may be appropriate:

Like thee, O forgiving Son, may I be martyred in thy martyrdom . . . .
may I suffer thy Passion with thee.

May I, in thy noble life, sacrifice to thee my life.
May I surrender my body in thy Body.
May I be poor in thy poverty.

So that I be like Mary in distress, may the seven keen shafts of sorrow for thy death pierce my heart like hers.

The thorns of his head, the spike in his footsoles,
the spear in his pap, the nail in his palms —
may these wound me, O God
tho' it be not enough to pay for thy blood.

May I bear the cross beside thee, may I drink thy drink of gall;
tho' to drink it were dire poison to me,
may I sit with thee at one banquet.[31]

The feeding-ground for the strong Christocentric and Marian devotion
was, of course, the sacred scriptures. The Patrician tradition of the Celtic
Church, a tradition for direct recourse to the scriptures, remained strong
from the Norman invasion to the Reformation and the following excerpt from the fourteenth-century Leabhar Breac (Speckled Book), is
but one of many testaments to the strength and quality of that tradition:

> One of the noble gifts of the Holy Spirit is the Holy Scriptures, by
> which all ignorance is enlightened and all worldly afflictions com-
> forted; by which all spiritual light is kindled and all debility is made
> strong. For it is through the Holy Scriptures that heresy and schism
> are banished from the Church, and all contentions and divisions re-
> conciled. In it will well-tried counsel and appropriate instruction be
> found for every degree in the Church.[32]

A later poet may be forgiven for some poetic licence when he writes:
"The Old Testament and the New the Gael has in purity, and all that the
inspired Prophet spoke he remembers without a mistake."[33]

Arising from this familiarity with the scriptures, great stress was laid
on the concept of the Mystical Body of Christ. The Celtic Church era
abounds with references to the subject and always balances off personal
petition with universal need. The Leabhar Breac has the following pas-
sage in one of its many homilies:

> In three ways do the holy commentators understand the Body of
> Christ: the first Body is the humanity born from the Virgin Mary
> without loss to her virginity; the second Body is the holy Church,
> that is, the perfect assembly of all the believers whose head is the
> Saviour, Jesus Christ, Son of the living God; the third Body is the
> holy Scripture, in which is set forth the mystery of the Body and
> Blood of Christ.[34]

The most popular of Old Testament books, beyond shadow of doubt,
was "Psalms", and the term "three fifties" quickly became a popular
mode of designating and categorising, be it warriors, saints, birds,
prayers, or the one hundred and fifty Hail Marys which were recited
by those who for one reason or another could not join in singing the
psalms. Little wonder then that, with a strong Marian devotion and an
equally strong allegiance to the "three fifties" of psalms, the rosary
became so popular in Ireland.

Psalm 118 enjoyed immense prestige and popularity. Beginning with
the Latin word "Beati" and known in popular parlance as "The Biait",
it was said to be "better than every prayer . . . to save the soul from

demons".[35] As a prayer for the dead it was a great favourite as the following rather amusing tale from the fifteenth-century Book of Lismore attests:

> Máel Póil Úa Cineatha, the abbot of the monastery of Cill Beagáin had been discussing astrology with another monk. Afterwards in his sleep he saw coming towards him a gospel-nun [i.e. apparently, a nun under the guidance of a spiritual director or soul-friend] who had died six months before. She raised a great complaint. "How are things there woman?" said he. "Much you care," said she, "discussing astrology and not saying my requiem [ecndairc] . Woe to you", said she. "What requiem do you want from me, woman?" said he. "The Biait, of course," said she, "the Biait after the Biait, the Biait on the Biait, the Biait beneath (or above) the Biait", said she, all in one breath, demanding that the Biait be recited often for her. So that there is no requiem, except the Mass for the dead, that is held in greater honour by God than the Biait, as was said:

> > "The best of wealth on earth
> > and that a man give it up for his soul's sake,
> > yet is God more grateful to him
> > for the continual recital of the Biait."[36]

Reference to purgatory is rare in this period, while the term "leac na bpian" was used to describe both purgatory and hell. Both of these infernal penalty areas might be entered through a series of caves, the best known being the "Purgatory" on the island of Lough Derg.

Side by side with sound tradition and healthy faith, there were, of course, unhealthy elements, superstitions, undue credulity in regard to miracles, and some downright abuses particularly with regard to marriage. The Irish chieftains were given to much marrying,[37] some having at least four wives.[38] The motivation varied — love, lust, or practical politics. The Brehon Law allowed considerable latitude in these matters and the Christian Church does not seem to have made Herculean efforts to introduce any other system until the twelfth-century reform. While men were accused of changing their wives as often as a modern man might change his car, the women were sometimes well-matched for them, one of the most notable being Cabhlaigh Mór O'Connor who died in 1395. O'Connor was facetiously nicknamed "Port-na-dtrí-namhad" (The Haven of the Three Enemies) after a County Donegal placename, because she had married three warriors who were sworn enemies.[39] Nor were these her only consorts.

Concubinage, too, was common, not only among the laity but among the clergy. The practice among the latter did not cause undue scandal among lay folk, who themselves attached little stigma to either concubinage or illegitimacy,[40] partly because of a blurring of many of the distinctions between cleric and layman. But even in sin the palm must sometimes go to the cleric: one particular abbot of O'Dorney in Kerry, for example, was widely known to be the greatest fornicator in the region. The illegitimate offspring of the clergy, comprising a variety of churchmen – regular, secular, abbots, bishops, and in later times an occasional parson[41] – were frequently put forward for high office in the Church. Indeed, when Cardinal Orsini proposed, in the secret consistory of 17 October 1580, a man of illegitimate birth for the archbishopric of Tuam, in Co. Galway, Pope Gregory XIII remarked that Irish candidates usually described themselves as nobles and bastards.[42]

Though taking a rather cavalier approach to sexual mores, the Irish, both clerical and lay, took very seriously the age-old tradition of hospitality. References to it find place in papal documents in such phrases as "after the manner of his country",[43] "keep up hospitality which is wont, after the custom of the country",[44] and "maintain hospitality according to the Irish manner".[45] The various religious houses were as generous in their exercise of hospitality as their resources allowed. The abbot of St Brogan's in Co. Waterford, claimed in 1477 that he was accustomed to feed forty poor men and pilgrims at the monastery daily.[46] The tradition of monastic hospitality was well-rooted in the social tradition of the time, and probably got its great impetus from the Celtic Church's view that a welcome for any guest was a welcome for Christ himself. Summing up this theme, Canice Mooney, the noted Franciscan historian from whose writings I have drawn liberally, has this to say:

> Hospitality, in the very widest sense of that word, flourished almost to a fault. The poor and the pilgrim, the wandering scholar, scribe, the harpist, all found welcome, food, and lodging at the many houses of hospitality that dotted the countryside. The sick poor, the lepers (in the medieval sense) and the orphans were all fairly adequately catered for. Despite the rigidly stratified nature of Irish society, hardly any obstacle was placed in the way of the advancement in Church or society of individuals of poor or handicapped origins, provided they possessed ability and character.[47]

Penance and fasting were still strong at the end of the medieval period. Rising at night for the office or some other forms of vigil prayers was also practised. "At midnight", says a foreign traveller, "they [the Irish] rise for prayer and meditation, to which some give a full hour, others half an hour, and at the same hour they always light the fire."[48] A quatrain from the poems of the fifteenth-century poet, Tadhg Óg Ó hUiginn, shows that human weakness was always in the picture:

> I am slow to rise
> in time for matins;

pardon me this, setting it against
every cold night he [Dominic] rose.[49]

For the purposes of meditation there was no scarcity of home or
foreign material for those who could read Irish, Latin, English, or
French. Bibles, psalters, scripture commentaries, the "Summa" of St
Thomas and other compendia of theology were available; so too were
Henry VIII's defence of the seven sacraments, St Thomas More's *Utopia*,
and the same author's defence of pilgrimage — a best-seller in Ireland
surely. Widely-read, too, were devotional works such as the *Little
Flower of St Francis*, Ludolf of Saxony's life of Christ, Innocent III's
De Contemptu Mundi, and the most important sixteenth-century Irish
publication, *Beatha Colaim Cille* (Life of St Columcille), compiled by
Manus O'Donnell in 1532 at Port-na-dtrí-namhad. Surviving manu-
scripts from the sixteenth century also testify to firm devotion to St
Michael, guardian angels, the two St Johns, and the three women saints,
Mary Magdalen, Margaret of Antioch, and Catherine of Alexandria.

At the catechetical level, "there was an understanding that all children
should be taught by heart the Our Father, the Hail Mary, the Creed, the
Commandments, the precepts of the Church, and the names of the
seven deadly sins. A certain number were taught to read the psalter in
Latin, and the recitation of the penitential psalms seems to have been
fairly common practice".[50]

Summing up the pre-Reformation Irish Church, Fr Canice Mooney
says:

On the credit side there is evidence of robust faith, of high regard for
the pope as vicar of Christ, of a mental outlook almost inextricably
interwoven with the Christian way of life, of great personal devotion
to Christ, Our Lady and the saints, of friendly relations between
clergy and laity. Still on the credit side, but not beyond criticism in
all its aspects, is the tradition of asceticism, for instance in regard to
fast and abstinence, as well as deep reverence for the relics and images
of the saints, and the undertaking of toilsome pilgrimages.[51]

Turbulent though the centuries were in the medieval period, darker
clouds were gathering in the first half of the sixteenth century as the
Reformation broke over Europe and the Tudors of England set themselves the task of bringing Ireland to heel from a political and religious
viewpoint. As Europe divided on religious lines, Ireland would line up
with the Catholic nations and look to them and to the Pope himself for
both temporal and spiritual succour. An Irish bard (poet) named Cos-
telloe, during the reign of Elizabeth I, apostrophises Ireland in a very
beautiful poem called "Róisín Dubh", translated by James Clarence
Mangan under the title "Dark Rosaleen". It not only captures the spirit
of the age, but that of the centuries ahead.[52]

O my dark Rosaleen,
  Do not sigh, do not weep!
The priests are on the ocean green,
  They march along the deep.
There's wine from the royal Pope,
  Upon the ocean green;
And Spanish ale shall give you hope,
  My Dark Rosaleen!
  My own Rosaleen!
Shall glad your heart, shall give you hope,
Shall give you health, and help and hope.
  My dark Rosaleen.

Over hills, and thro' dales,
  Have I roam'd for your sake;
All yesterday I sail'd with sails
  On river and on lake.
The Erne, at its highest flood,
  I dashed across unseen,
For there was lightning in my blood,
  My Dark Rosaleen!
  My own Rosaleen!
O, there was lightning in my blood,
Red lightning lighten'd thro' my blood.
  My Dark Rosaleen!

All day long, in unrest,
  To and fro, do I move.
The very soul within my breast
  Is wasted for you, love!
The heart in my bosom faints
  To think of you, my Queen,
My life of life, my saint of saints,
  My Dark Rosaleen!
  My own Rosaleen!
To hear your sweet and sad complaints,
My life, my love, my saint of saints,
  My Dark Rosaleen!

Woe and pain, pain and woe,
  Are my lot, night and noon,
To see your bright face clouded so,
  Like to the mournful moon.
But yet will I rear your throne
  Again in golden sheen;

'Tis you shall reign, shall reign alone,
  My Dark Rosaleen!
  My own Rosaleen!
'Tis you shall have the golden throne,
'Tis you shall reign, and reign alone,
  My dark Rosaleen!

Over dews, over sands,
  Will I fly, for your weal;
Your holy delicate white hands
  Shall girdle me with steel.
At home, in your emerald bowers,
  From morning's dawn till e'en,
You'll pray for me, my flower of flowers,
  My Dark Rosaleen!
  My fond Rosaleen!
You'll think of me through daylight hours,
My virgin flower, my flower of flowers,
  My Dark Rosaleen!

I could scale the blue air,
  I could plough the high hills,
O, I could kneel all night in prayer,
  To heal your many ills!
And one beamy smile from you
  Would float like light between
My toils and me, my own, my true,
  My Dark Rosaleen!
  My fond Rosaleen!
Would give me life and soul anew,
A second life, a soul anew,
  My Dark Rosaleen!

O, the Erne shall run red,
  With redundance of blood,
The earth shall rock beneath our tread,
  And flames wrap hill and wood,
And gun-peal and slogan-cry
  Wake many a glen serene,
Ere you shall fade, ere you shall die,
  My Dark Rosaleen!
  My own Rosaleen!
The Judgment Hour must first be nigh,
Ere you can fade, ere you can die,
  My Dark Rosaleen!

4 "Irish and Catholic"

During the sixteenth century, religion was to become the burning question in Ireland as elsewhere in Europe. Nevertheless, the Reformation came somewhat as a surprise in Ireland as the Irish Church did not feel the pressures that seemed to be influencing the Church in Germany, for example.

Among the old Gaelic stock of the late medieval period, there was a strong faith, though good works were not always in such abundant supply. The same may be said of the new Anglo-Norman nobility. In 1504, for example, Gerald Fitzgerald, the Great Earl of Kildare, burned down the cathedral at Cashel. On being censured for his action, the only excuse he offered was that he thought the archbishop was in it.[1]

But the faith showed itself in a realistic facing of facts regarding repentance and the world to come. It was not uncommon for members of the nobility to end their days in repentance within the walls of a monastery, while petitioning to be clothed at death in the religious habit of the friars was common among all strata of society. All wanted to die "after unction and penance",[2] while every poet worthy of the name, but who in his heyday may not have been a paragon of "gospel-living", would nevertheless, when the end was drawing near, sit down and write his "aithrí" − his poem of repentance. One and all shared a belief in the mercy of God rather than a dread of his anger, and believed further that the Mother of God would put in a good word on their behalf in the right place and at the right time.

Nor did the Irish have any grievance about the scriptures being witheld from them because in practice they were not. The literate could read the Latin Vulgate or *Meditationes Vitae Christi*. At the same time, both preachers and vernacular devotional works gave practical instruction based on scripture stories and themes which had been told and retold in tradition from the beginnings of Irish Christianity.

As far as strained relations with the Pope were concerned, Canice Mooney captures the Irish attitude admirably when he says: "Far from feeling any resentment about papal aggression, the average native Irishman of standing or education welcomed the fact that over and above the king of England stood the common father of Christendom, to whom in the last resort all could appeal for justice."[3]

Consequently, the Irish had virtually no interest in Martin Luther or his propositions, while Luther for his part never refers to Ireland, though his youth cannot be devoid of Irish associations, since he studied law at Erfurt, an ancient Irish Benedictine foundation, about which Nicholas de Bibera wrote in his *Carmen Satiricum:*

> Sunt et ibi [in Erfurt] Scoti
> qui cum fuerint bene poti,
> Sanctum Brendanum
> proclamant esse decanum
> in grege sanctorum
> vel quod deus ipse deorum
> Brendanus frater
> Sit et ejus Brigida mater.
> Sed vulgus miserum
> non credens hoc esse verum,
> estimat insanos
> Scotos simul atque profanos.[4]

In free translation it runs something like this:

> There are those Irishmen [in Erfurt]
> who, when high on alcohol
> proclaim that Brendan is Chief
> of the flock of the blessed,
> or that God Almighty Himself
> is Brendan's brother,
> and Brigid His Mother.
> But the ordinary man in the street
> not believing this to be true,
> judges the Irish to be
> both irreverent and daft.

As far as Ireland was concerned, then, we may say that the Reformation on the Continent was a non-event.

Not so the Reformation in England. There were already wide differences between Ireland and England in matters of language, culture and tradition. Tudor absolutism could not tolerate a further widening of the chasm between the two nations. A change of religion in England demanded similar action in Ireland. Right through the sixteenth century, therefore, the Tudor monarchs pursued a relentless campaign of violence, treachery, diplomacy, and any other method calculated to advance the anglicisation of Ireland.

In August 1589, Arthur Lord Grey came to Ireland as head of the queen's forces and earned for himself a niche in history as one of Europe's and the world's most barbarous tyrants. Edmond Spencer, the Elizabethan poet, himself no angel of light, accompanied Grey on many campaigns, including the devastation of Munster. But even Spencer saw the futility of scorched-earth policies and wrote: "Complaint was made against him [Grey], that he was a bloodie man, and regarded not the life of her subjects no more than dogges, but had wasted and consumed all, so as now she had nothing almost left, but to raigne in their ashes."[5] One of the numerous victims of the campaign was the papal legate, Dr Nicholas Saunders, who, after many hair-breadth escapes, eventually fell victim to starvation: "His body afterwards found in a roadside hovel, mangled since death by the attacks of wild beasts, whose ordinary ferocity were rendered desperate by the general destruction of the usual production of nature".[6]

The war proceeded until both the Old Gaelic and Anglo-Norman nobility were gradually brought to their knees, the battle of Kinsale in 1601 delivering the final death-blow to the old Irish world.

Subverting the ancient faith in Ireland was, however, a far more formidable task than it had been in England, where resentment had been growing against the Church. No such popular resentment existed in Ireland.[7] But the people of Ireland, as well as elsewhere in Europe, were frequently confused and there are many examples of outward conformity through ignorance or merely following the line of least resistance. "The catholic practice of outwardly conforming, so prevalent in the time of James I, was the occasion in the following reign for issuing a Bull by Pope Urban VIII in which the people, who, in spite of previous papal condemnation, had hitherto attended Anglican services without scruple, were exhorted to suffer death rather than continue to do so."[8]

In Ireland the people had faith and religious zeal but "the Irish laity were still for the most part only passively and traditionally catholic, and had not yet been roused to that passionate devotion to their religion for which they were remarkable during the next two centuries".[9] The old religion, professed by the Anglo-Norman and Gaelic Irish alike, soon disclosed itself as a force making for Irish unity, and for resistance to England.[10] As early as 1539, we find complaints that friars "do preach daily that every man ought, for the salvation of his soul, fight and make war against our sovereign lord the king's majesty, and if any of them die in the quarrel his soul . . . shall go to Heaven, as the souls of SS. Peter, Paul and others, who suffer death and martyrdom for God's sake".[11]

As the idea of nationality evolved in Europe and Church and State tended to find their separate levels, the elements of nationality and catholicity tended to blend in Ireland. In fact, they became virtually synonymous, and the word "English" was often used to denote "Protestant", even though the family might have been established in Ireland for generations. Indeed, as McLysaght points out and my personal experience corroborates, the words "Protestant" and "Sasanach" (Englishman) are frequently interchangeable.[12]

It is a curious thing that the Catholic community in England, who were a severely persecuted minority, were never well-disposed towards

Ireland or its suffering people. This spirit survives into the late twentieth century but in the seventeenth it was less covert. D'Avaux, writing to Louis XIV in April 1689, remarks "Les Irlandois reconnoissent aussi que les Anglois qui sont aupres du roi, meme les Catholiques, son leurs plus grand ennemis."[13] (The Irish also recognise that the English who are close to the king, even the Catholics, are their greatest enemies.) A letter of Bishop O'Moloney's, which Archbishop King thought worth quoting, supports this view. He says: "Nor is there any Englisman, Catholic or other, of what quality or degree soever alive will stick to sacrifice all Ireland for to save the least interest of his own in England; and would as willingly see all Ireland over inhabited by English of whatsoever religion, as by the Irish."[14]

In the middle of the seventeenth century, Oliver Cromwell, the personification of Puritan fanaticism, arrived in Ireland. He left his permanent mark by a series of massacres. In his onslaught on the traditional faith, Cromwell struck right at the heart of the matter by viciously attacking the Mass, so that when a town was captured, the clergy were almost invariably excluded from pardon.[15] "I meddle not with any man's conscience," he wrote on 19 October 1649 when demanding the surrender of New Ross, "but if by liberty of conscience you mean a liberty to exercise the Mass, I judge it best to use plain dealing, and let you know where the parliament of England have power, that will not be allowed of".[16] The author of Cambrensis Eversus elaborates a little on the doleful aftermath:

> Under the Protectorate it was death to harbour or protect a priest; death not to disclose their hiding-places "in the caverns of the mountains, the chasms of the quarry, and in the dark recesses of the forest". And "any person accidentally meeting and recognising a priest was subject to have his ears cut off, and to be flogged naked through the town, if he did not inform". "Many a time", says Bruodin, "were these iniquitious laws enforced in Ireland."[17]

Despite the all-out and ruthlessly systematic attempt on the part of the Puritans to exterminate Catholicism in Ireland, their efforts were without any real success. "The religious conservatism of the people, the fact that the reformed religion was associated with an alien government, and the missionary efforts of the agents of the counter-reformation . . . all combined to entrench Catholicism."[18] John Wesley assessed the situation after half a century of anti-Catholic rule:

> At least ninety-nine in a hundred of the native Irish remained in the religion of their forefathers. The Protestants whether in Dublin or elsewhere are almost all transplanted from England. Nor is it any wonder that those who are born Papists generally live and die such, when the Protestants can find no better way to convert them than penal laws and acts of parliament.[19]

The transplanting from England of which John Wesley spoke went on at a considerable pace and repeated efforts were made when schemes failed. "To Hell or to Connaught", the famed remark attributed to Cromwell, effectively ordered that all Catholics be exterminated or forced to live in a ghetto — the ghetto in this instance being the province of Connaught, the least fertile and productive of the four provinces of Ireland. But the Cromwellian interpretation of "Irish" was even more interesting. It embraced, for all practical purposes, anybody living on the island who professed the Catholic faith, including many English settlers who looked on themselves as anything but Irish. This practical division cemented the concepts of "Irish" and "Catholic". The towns which had traditional loyalties outside of Ireland and perpetual hostility towards the inhabitants of the rural hinterland suddenly found common cause with their neighbours, because the inhabitants of the towns remained fiercely loyal to the old faith — Carrickfergus being the only town in the country to go over officially to the Protestant religion. It is a curious quirk of fate that "the union of Catholics in Ireland was, from first to last, a Protestant achievement, not a Catholic one".[20]

The extent of the importation or "planting" of Protestants from England, Scotland, Wales and the Continent may be measured in terms of land confiscated from the Catholic community, as indicated in the following table:[21]

1530 Catholics owned 100% of the land
1641   „   „   59% „ „ „
1703   „   „   14% „ „ „
1778   „   „   5% „ „ „

Property and privilege rather than religion were at the root of much of the persecution of Catholics. Thus, for the most part, the penal sanctions were aimed at despoiling the Catholic population at the levels of property, faith, language and tradition.

The legal inducements offered to Catholics to change their religion were based, not on spiritual values, but on personal ambition to climb the social ladder, or retain, at least in part, hereditary estates. Yet converts from Gaelic stock were few, and fewer still made the religious transition with a clear conscience. The case of the Gaelic poet, Piaras Mac Gearailt (1700-1791) is typical of the uneasy conscience:

'Tis sad for me to cleave to Calvin or perverse Luther, but the weeping of my children, the spoiling them of flocks and land brought streaming floods from my eyes and descent of tears . . . There is a part of the Saxon Lutheran religion which, though not from choice, I have accepted that I do not like — that never a petition is addressed to Mary, the mother of Christ, nor honour nor privilege nor prayer, and yet it is my opinion that it is Mary who is . . . tree of lights and crystal of Christianity, the glow and precious lantern of the sky, the sunny chamber in the house of glory, flood of graces and Cliona's wave of mercy.[22]

Though failing to destroy Catholicism, the Puritans did succeed in establishing a permanent Protestant ascendancy: those planters whom the Munster poet, Ó Bruadair, styles "rogues formed from the dregs of each base trade, who range themselves snugly in the houses of the noblest chiefs, as proud and genteel as if sons of gentlemen".[23] Lecky, the noted and unusually perceptive historian of the times, does not see a mere amorphus mob of squalid, ignorant "papists" in their mud cabins — a level beyond which many of his contemporaries and countrymen did not see. Instead he has glimpses of that other Ireland in which "ejected proprietors whose names might be traced in the Annals of the Four Masters, or around the sculptured crosses of Clonmacnoise might be found in abject poverty hanging around the land that had lately been their own, shrinking from servile labour as from an intolerable pollution and still receiving a secret homage from their old tenants".[24]

The ascendancy class had no real desire to convert the "papists", as Catholics were disparagingly designated, for their ambition was to corner as much wealth as possible among the smallest number of people. Lecky puts it in a sentence: "It was intended to make them [the Irish Catholics] poor and to keep them poor, to crush them in every germ of enterprise, to degrade them into a servile caste who could never hope to rise to the level of their oppressors."[25] No wonder that McLysaght could bluntly state in his *Irish Life in the Seventeenth Century:*

> The penal laws enacted against Irish catholics in the eighteenth century may be regarded as the worst in the annals of religious intolerance, not only because they were devised at a date when the world had freed itself from medieval ideas, but also because in themselves they were infamous, relying as they did on treachery and dishonour for their execution and being imposed on the majority by a minority, powerful only by reason of external backing.[26]

Here was the rub. The persecution of Protestants in France and Spain was cited to justify the savage laws now passed against Irish Catholics, but in those countries the members of the persecuted sect formed only a small minority, while Ireland was unique in that the persecuted formed the majority of the population. Furthermore, the minority relied on the military force of England to operate the barbarous system.

The effect of the penal laws on the people was interesting. Among other things, it led to a heightening of the faith, a strengthening of conviction, a revealing, through suffering and deprivation, of the real value the people placed on their creed and particularly on the Mass. There was further strengthening of the links between "Irish" and "Catholic" for, stripped of political power and ownership of the land, the people came to see their Catholic faith as having another property, namely, that of giving them an identity which the persecutor could not take away. Indeed, the more intense the persecution grew, the more the persecutor helped to forge identity between the Irishman's faith and fatherland. As early as 1625, one John Roche from New Ross quotes a Protestant source to the effect that "the very ground the Irish tread, the air they breathe, the climate they share, the very sky above them, all seem to draw them to the religion of Rome, so much so that if one of them appears to abandon it the very enemies of the Catholic Faith doubt his sincerity".[27]

In the first half of the seventeenth century, prior to the Puritan assault, the Church had some breathing space in which the hierarchy was strengthened and religious orders, especially the Franciscans, expanded. Many young men went to the Continent where they received education for the priesthood in one of the newly-founded "Irish Colleges". This link with the Continent was a real lifeline for the faith in Ireland during the dark days ahead.

After the failure of the forces of the Confederation of Kilkenny to overcome the Puritans in the mid-seventeenth century, France again became a haven. In 1652, through Cardinal Mazarin's diplomacy, 20,000 men of the Confederate army in Ireland were transferred to the army of France. A considerable number of proscribed priests also settled in France, especially in Paris. Fr Vincent de Paul extended his kindly hand to aid those who suffered much hardship. Some became *curés*, while others crowded into the schools and universities where their talent and scholarship were recognised and rewarded. Indicative of the age is the fact that the office of Procurator of the German Nation of the University of Paris was practically the monopoly of Irishmen from beginning to end of the seventeenth century. The "German Nation" here meant students and scholars from northern and north-eastern Europe.[28] The French king did his part for the exiles, as the recreant Lord O'Brien, himself an Irishman, testifies: "All the youth of that kingdom [Ireland] are sent over into France where they are bred up to the Church, Law or Sword . . . the French king keeps above 2,000 always in colleges for divinity and law and has now for the most part in his service all those whose estates were forfeited."[29] Such information from O'Brien was sad reading indeed for the English government to whom it was sent, as England was now feeling the effects of the "Irish Brigade", already becoming legendary for its spirit and reckless bravery. The King of France, on the other hand, must have felt generously repaid for patronage bestowed on the exiles: in approximately half a century (1700-1750), two hundred thousand Irishmen gave their lives on Continental battlefields — chiefly in the service of France.

Of all the centuries of Irish history, perhaps the eighteenth is the saddest. Stripped of every vestige of human dignity which the destroyer could remove, the people were ground into the dust. But as the trampling of the grape produces the wine, so the grinding of the common people brought to the surface the riches and inner resources of their faith. The result was a tremendous blossoming of popular piety in the form of folk-prayers which fed the spiritual life of the people. These prayers, together with the rosary and the very occasional Mass which was celebrated at the peril of life and in the remotest of places, gave strength to an already religious people.

In 1974 Fr Diarmaid Ó Laoghaire, SJ, published a collection of five hundred and thirty-nine folk-prayers. It is not an exhaustive collection, nor is it the only collection, but it is indicative of the riches of popular piety to find that so many have survived. Neither the authorship nor the date of composition is known in most cases, but the seventeenth and eighteenth centuries can perhaps lay claim to very many of them. A glance at the contents page indicates the wide range: prayers rising in the morning, to one's guardian angel (a personage so familiar in the Gaelic world that when saluting a single person the plural form is often used, i.e. to include the guardian angel), prayers before and after meals, of repentance, before work, before a journey, at time of death; a host of prayers associated with the rosary of Mary, with the passion of Christ, with the Holy Spirit, the Eternal Father and the Trinity; prayers to Christ in his glory, to the saints, and a host of others; but the longest list of all is a collection of close on a hundred beautiful prayers con cerning the Mass. [30]

From *Our Mass our Life*, another of Fr Ó Laoghaire's publications, I give a sample of prayers connected with the Mass. It is difficult to make a choice due to the beauty of each. In the original Irish these prayers are for the most part in verse. The first example is a prayer, from Kerry, to be recited on the way to Mass:

> Siúlaimid mar aon leis an Maighdin Mhuire
> agus leis na daoine naofa eile a bhí ag
> tionlacadh a haon-Mhic ar Chnoc Calbharaí.
>
> (We walk together with the Virgin Mary
> and the other holy people who accompanied her only Son
> on the Hill of Calvary.)[31]

Another beautiful prayer to the "Rí an Domhnaigh bheannaithe" (King of the blessed Sunday) is my next choice. The term "King of the blessed Sunday" is a warm and very familiar title in Gaelic, corresponding to the scriptural "Kurios" (the risen Lord). This prayer was associated with a special "coróin" or rosary:

> Céad fáilte romhat, a Rí an Domhnaigh bheannaithe
> do tháinig le cabhair chugainn tar éis na seachtaine.

Corraigh mo chos go moch chun Aifrinn,
corraigh im béal na bréithre beannaithe,
corraigh mo chroí agus díbir an ghangaid as.
Féachaim suas ar Mhac trócaireach,
mar is é is fearr a cheannaigh shinn
agus gur leis féin beo is marbh sinn.

(A hundred welcomes to thee, O King of Blessed Sunday
who has come to help us after the week.
My feet guide early to Mass,
part my lips with blessed words,
stir up my heart and banish out of it all spite.
I look up to the Son of the Nurse,
her one and only Son of Mercy,
for He it is who has so excellently redeemed us
and His we are whether we live or die).[32]

That prayer was said on the large beads of the rosary and the following
on the small beads:

V. Céad fáilte romhat, a Rí an Domhnaigh ghlórmhair.
A Mhic na hÓighe is a Rí na Glóire,

R. A Íosa mhilis is a Mhic Mhuire,
déan trócaire orainn.

V. (A hundred welcomes to you, O King of glorious Sunday.
O Son of the Virgin and King of Glory,

R. O sweet Jesus, O Son of Mary,
have mercy on us.)[33]

Then on sight of the church or entering it:

Is beannaithe Teach Dé
is beannaím féin dó.
Mar a bhfuil sé leis an dá aspal déag.
Go mbeannaí Mac Dé dúinn.
Is beannaithe thú, a Athair bheannaithe,
is beannaithe thú, a Mhic an Athair bheannaithe,
is beannaithe thú, a Theampaill an Spioraid Naoimh,
is beannaithe thú, a Eaglais na Tríonóide.

(Blessed is the House of God
and I myself greet him
where he is with the twelve apostles.
May the Son of God bless us.
Blessed are you, O holy Father,
Blessed are you, O Son of the holy Father,
Blessed are you, O Temple of the Holy Spirit,
Blessed are you, O Church of the Trinity.)[34]

Greetings extended to the altar, the symbol of the cross and the crucified, are set in another versified prayer:

Go mbeannaíthear duit, a altóir,
a chros bhreá dhuilliurach ghlas.
Nár lige tú m'anam thart;
go gcoinní tú mé ar dea-staid,
go bhfuille tú sinne ar ár leas,
go méadaí tú ár gcroí le glóir a fháil,
go líona tú ár súile le deora na haithrí,
go dtuga tú ár gcion dúinn de gach Aifreann
dá léitear sa Róimh inniu
agus ar fud an domhain mhóir. Amen.

(Hail to you, O altar,
O beautiful, flowering, green cross,
let not my soul pass you by.
May you keep me in the state of grace,
may you convert us to the right way,
may you enlarge our hearts to be filled with glory,
may you fill our eyes with tears of repentance,
may you give us our share of every Mass
that is celebrated in Rome today
and throughout the whole world. Amen.)[35]

Reference to Christ as the "poor crucified rider" is common in Irish prayers, the notion of Christ riding the cross being a familiar image in high-class Irish poetry of several centuries prior to the days of persecution. Common, too, are references to the universal Church and above all to Rome. The Mother of God is frequently mentioned in these prayers and a great number of prayers are in the plural because of a keen awareness of the community of God's people, the Body of Christ.

A little quatrain comes down to us giving a Gaelic notion of the people's ideal of a priest:

B'áil liom sagart breá sultarach pléisiúrtha,
lán de chreideamh is carthanach nádúrtha,
a bheadh báidheach le bochtaibh is cneasta lena thréadaí,
ach níorbh áil liom stollaire fé chulaith mhín an Aon-Mhic.

(I would like a fine, pleasant, cheerful priest,
full of faith, charitable and kindly,
who would have sympathy for the poor and be gentle with his flock,
but I would not like a good-for-nothing in the fair livery of the
    Only Son.)[36]

Fr Diarmuid Ó Laoghaire pertinently compares this peasant verse with the ideal proposed in the Vatican II decree on the ministry and life of priests: "priests will find great help in the possession of those virtues which are deservedly esteemed in human affairs, such as goodness of heart, sincerity, strength and constancy of character, civility . . ."[37]

For every part of the Mass the people had not one but several beautiful prayers. In such a work as this I can do little more than refer my readers to the sources.[38] However, I cannot refrain from quoting a little more. The following is a translation of a "welcoming prayer" after the Consecration:

> A hundred thousand welcomes, thou Body of the Lord,
> Thou Son of her the Virgin, the brightest, most adorned,
> > Thy death in such fashion
> > On the tree of the Passion
> Hath saved Eve's race and put sin to death.
>
> I am a poor sinner to thee appealing,
> > Reward me not as my sins may be;
> O Jesus Christ I deserve Thy anger,
> > But turn again and show grace to me.
>
> Jesus who bought us,
> Jesus who taught us,
> > Jesus of the united prayer [i.e. the rosary],
> > Do not forget us
> Now nor in the hour of death.
>
> O crucified Jesus, do not leave us,
> Thou pourdest Thy blood for us, O forgive us,
> May the Grace of the Spirit for ever be with us,
> And whatever we ask may the Son of God give us.[39]

The joy and the welcome at the Consecration of the Mass was phenomenal. Even into the twentieth century the remoter and more thoroughly Gaelic areas reflected a certain after-glow of the genuine Gaelic piety. Eilís Ní Chorra describes a Mass she attended in Achill, Co. Mayo, early in the century:

> The church was packed and never before (or since) have I seen and heard such fervour. The congregation attended Mass in every sense of the word, making the responses aloud with the altar boys, and at the Consecration there was such a cry of welcome to our Lord in the Blessed Sacrament — "Céad míle fáilte, a Thiarna" (a hundred thousand welcomes Lord) — that the tears came to my eyes — and I am not an emotional person.[40]

To Owen Roe O'Sullivan, the eighteenth-century poet and darling lyricist of Munster, is attributed this beautiful version of the Our Father:

Ár nAthair atá ar Neamh
do cheap sinn féin ar dtúis,
go naomhaíthear t'ainm
is go dtagaimid go léir id dhún,
t'aon-toil bheannaithe
ar an dtalamh go ndéanam súd
fé mar dheineann gach neach ar Neamh
nuair a théid id dhún.
An t-arán geal do cheapais féin dúinn tabhair
is ár gcionta ar fad go maithir féinig dúinn,
fé mar a mhaith an Mac don fhear gan néall 'na shúil,
Ná lig sinn sa ríocht san as nach féidir teacht,
in aon drochní na i dtintibh daora i dteas,
ach amen, a Chríost, agus lig sinn go léir isteach.

(Our Father who art in Heaven
who fashioned us in the beginning,
may your name be made holy
and may we all enter your house,
your holy and only will
may we do it on earth
as does everyone in Heaven who enters in.
Give the bright bread you made for us,
and all our sins may you yourself forgive
as the Son forgave the man of the sightless eyes.
Do not let us enter the kingdom of the dead
in a state of sin, nor into the heat of hell's fires,
but amen, O Christ, do you admit us all.)[41]

There was a custom, still is perhaps, of taking a drink — or three sips — of water after Holy Communion. Here is an accompanying prayer from Mayo and Kerry:

Sláinte an Ard-Mhic do leath a ghéaga
ar chrann na Páise chun sinn a shaoradh
agus sláinte na mná mánla do rug a Mac gan chéile
agus sláinte Naomh Pádraig do bheannaigh Éire.

(Health to the noble Son who spread his arms
on the tree of the Passion to free us,
and health to the gentle woman who without man gave birth to her Son,
and health to Saint Patrick who blessed Ireland.)[42]

Fidelity to the Mass was the aspect of the faith which outshone all other expressions of it in the penal times. The seventeenth and eighteenth centuries were noted as the age of the Mass-rock. It was the age of the "Sagart Aroon" (the darling priest), as the people affectionately designated their pastor. They sheltered him at the risk of life and limb; by night he ministered to them and, in the remote caves and bogs, in a shack or beside a fence or on a boulder or rock, he would celebrate the outlawed Mass. Secret signs passed from one to another across the countryside would signal the time of sacrifice, so that those who could not risk being present could join in the spirit at the exact time of celebration.

But these centuries were also the age of the priest-hunter, the most infamous being perhaps John Garzia, an Iberian Jew, and Edward Tyrrell, a renegade Catholic executed in 1713 for bigamy. In a surviving manuscript of Dr Nicholas Madgett, Bishop of Kerry from 1753 to 1774, we learn that the following scale of reward obtained in his day:

£30.00 sterling or current money for a simple priest;
£50.00 for a bishop;
£40.00 for a vicar-general;
£50.00 for a Jesuit.[43]

The loathing of the people for the priest-hunter is typified in a quatrain by poet Tadhg Ó Neachtain, on the occasion of seeing the body of Tyrell hanging on the gibbet:

Maith do thoradh, a chrainn!
Rath do thoraidh ar gach aon chraoibh:
Truagh gan crainnte Inse Fáil
Lán ded' thoradh gach aon lá!

(Good is thy fruit O tree!
The luck of thy fruit on every bough;
Would that all the trees of Ireland
Were full of thy fruit every single day!)[44]

While there were exceptions, the behaviour of the clergy in the persecution was admirable. "We shall not abandon our flocks", wrote St Oliver Plunkett, primate and martyr, "till we are compelled by force to do so: we will first suffer imprisonment and other torments. We have already suffered so much on the mountains, in huts and caverns, and we have acquired such a habit that for the future suffering will be less severe and troublesome."[45] John Brennan, Bishop of Waterford and Lismore, writing in June 1672, informs us that no bishop had been seen in many parts of his diocese for forty years, and that confirmation was being administered to people up to sixty years of age.[46] A few months later, in his report to Rome, he says: "the people, generally speaking are very religious and pious, leading a Christian life without great fault or many scandals. They are most devoted (tenacissimi) to the Catholic faith and have great reverence for the Apostolic See."[47] The closeness between clergy and people was always there but in the days of common misfortune it grew stronger as the people who had lost all saw that the priest was willing to share their plight and minister to them in their misery. A traditional ballad captures the spirit:

> Who in the winter night, Sagart Aroon,
> When the cold blast did bite, Sagart Aroon,
> Came to my cabin door,
> And on the earthen floor,
> Knelt by me, sick and poor,
> Sagart Aroon.

Of course, the oppressed Irish did not rely wholly on bended knees for survival. The *bon Dieu* had given them a sharp, quick wit and, whether or not he meant it to be thus used, the Irishman often employed this gift for purposes of immersing the enemy in oceans of withering satire. One of the most celebrated quatrains of the period sets out a comparison between the foundation-stone of the Catholic Church and the foundation-stone of the Protestant (Anglican) Church. It has done more to boost Catholic morale and demolish the credibility of the "Reformed" Church than a thousand eloquent sermons or learned discourses:

> Ná trácht ar an mhinistéir gallda
> Ná ar a chreidcamh gan beann, gan bhrí,
> Mar níl mar bhuan-chloch dá theampuill,
> Ach magairlí Aonraoi Rí

Literally, it means "Don't speak of the alien minister, nor of his faith without rhyme or reason, for there is no foundation-stone to his Church except the testicles of Henry the King." Brendan Behan, the twentieth-century Irish playwright, gives the translation a little more than a metrical turn:

> Don't speak of the alien minister,
> Nor of his church without meaning or faith,
> For the foundation-stone of his temple
> Is the bollocks of Henry the Eighth.[48]

With such sentiments as these imbedded in the race-memory, one may be justified in concluding that ecumenical dialogue in Ireland may take a little longer than elsewhere.

At the catechetical level, *Parrthas an Anama* (Paradise of the Soul) was published by a Franciscan named Anton Gearnon in 1645 and widely used over the following centuries. An idea of its tone and content may be gleaned from the following excerpt from chapter eight:

Q. What should the Christian do at midnight?
A. He should perform matins and say the canonical hours or the Hours of Mary or the Crown of Jesus or the Rosary or the Litanies

of Jesus, Mary or the saints or any prayer for the souls in purgatory; in addition he should spend some time thinking on the Passion of Christ, on his last end and on the souls in hell and in purgatory who sleep not, but are being burned in unquenchable fires. Let him consider likewise that the angels and saints in heaven are not sleeping, but are for ever praising God, and let him imitate them especially at that time; for there is no better time for prayer than that, since the mind is then quiet and at rest and free from worldly care and trouble.

Q. Is there any other reason besides that for making these prayers at midnight rather than at any other time?

A. Yes: firstly, because at that hour Christ was born and also, according to some of the holy fathers, will come to judgment. As well as that, in the Old Testament it was customary to pray at that time, whence the Psalmist and King, David, says that although many things demanded his attention: "Media nocte surgebam ad confitendum tibi" (Ps. 118 − I rise at midnight to give praise to thee). Christ our Lord taught the same thing in the New Testament, as we find in St Luke the Evangelist in the 6th. c. "Erat Iesus pernoctans in oratione Dei", i.e. Jesus spent the night in prayer; and most of the saints of the Church imitated Him in this matter.This fine custom is still kept up as a rule by the religious Orders and by other holy people. It is not long since the same holy practice was common throughout Ireland among all sorts of people who loved God and had a care for the health of their souls.[49]

Side by side with the occasional Mass and instruction and the handing on of a living faith from parents to their children, the people nourished their faith further through a succession of religious feasts − pilgrimages to holy wells or other hallowed spots, pattern days (from "patron"), fasts, and many other age-old expressions of a people given to celebration.

The pilgrimage to Lough Derg was, of course, a special occasion, and the pilgrims brought home crosses (nowadays known as "penal crosses" − from the persecution days) as souvenirs, inscribed with the date of their visit. Pilgrimages were forbidden by law but the chief opposition was later to come from some of the Catholic bishops and clergy − a point dealt with more fully in the next chapter. Despite the legal prohibition of the oppressor, the pilgrimage and pattern refused to die. It was too deeply rooted in the cultural background of the people, a real need in their lives. In 1609, Sir Arthur Chichester complained to the privy council that Jesuits and priests from abroad flocked to Inishgaltaghe (Inish Cealtra on the Shannon) "to give absolution and pardons, and they come and go hence with the swallows . . . making a yearly revenue of poor and rich".[50] This particular centre for pilgrimage came to an end as a religious gathering-place of note in 1839, because, as Professor O'Donovan notes, "some ill-behaved young rascals" took to the habit of carrying off young girls by force from the crowd thus providing themselves with "fresh consorts for the ensuing year".[51]

Fasting — even in these "bad old days" — was not neglected, and Dr Madgett in his *Constitutio Ecclesiastica* wonders about the official Church fasts and the popular notion of fast: "What is to be thought", he poses, "of the old way of fasting among our country-people, what they call 'black fast' (dobh Carise) i.e. they take two full meals without meat, eggs or any kind of milk-meats, only bread, water and pottage or very rarely ale?"[52]

The passion of Christ, too, is a constant companion and it must have provided consolation for the people in their own hour of trial. Here is one popular prayer on the subject:

O Lord, Thou wast tortured on Friday,
And wast crucified on the cross of pain,
Thou wast tightly bound with chords,
And wast given to drink
A draught of bitter-tasting gall.
But, thanks to God, Thy persecutors failed;
Thou didst save the countless thousands
Whom the fiends held in bondage,
And to whom day was as night
Until they went to the brightness of Paradise
Where they found sweet music and delights,
And a mantle white with which to clothe the King and His host. Amen.[53]

And here is another prayer, one to be said on Friday night when lying on one's bed:

A Rígh an Aoine
Do shín do ghéuga ar an gcroich
A Thighearna ar ar fhulaing tú
Na mílte agus na céudta lot
Sínimid síos
Faoi dhídean do sgéithe anocht
Agus go sgapaidh tú orainn toradh an chroinn
Ar céusadh air do chorp. Amen.[54]

(O King of the Friday,
Whose limbs on the cross were bound;
O Lord, Who didst suffer
Sharp pain in many a wound;
We lay down to rest
Beneath the shield of Thy might,
May fruit from the tree
Of Thy Passion fall on us this night. Amen.)[55]

And yet another prayer brings out the warmth and concern for those members of the Body of Christ who have passed into the world beyond. In translation from the Gaelic it runs:

> We offer up a Pater and an Ave in honour of God and the Virgin Mary for the poor souls who are suffering the pains of Purgatory, and especially for the souls of our own relations; for every poor soul for whom there is none to pray; for every soul in great and urgent need; for the soul that has last departed from this world, and for every poor soul burdened with the guilt of an imperfect confession, a forgotten Mass, or a penance not performed. We include them all in this prayer: may God release them to-night. Amen.[56]

I do not know the date of composition of this prayer but it may be of nineteenth-century origin. The sentiments expressed are most familiar to me from childhood. It may well be a prayer forming part of "the trimmings of the rosary" — that litany of prayers for a variety of intentions which was part of the prayer-life of virtually every household in the country.

With a certain easing of the persecution in the eighteenth century, people began to grow bolder in asserting their right to worship. All over the land there sprang up little Mass-houses, in town and country alike, and to these hovels the people would resort. Though I cannot give the reference, I once read of a John Mezzafalce, a missionary returning from China on an English ship. In the first decade of the eighteenth century he found himself weatherbound for months off the west coast of Ireland, at Galway. Giving his testimony as an eyewitness in a letter to the Pope, he spoke of the

> constancy and devotedness with which they [the Irish] adhered to the Holy See . . . though they were ridiculed and laughed at yet they all faithfully observed the fast and abstinence . . . In order to hear Mass on Sundays and holydays, the men and women go out from the city, for Mass is not permitted within the city walls . . . This constancy amid so many persecutions is quite general and shared by almost all of every condition and sex and age . . .

Finally, a little bit of fun and humour has always been a great support to the Irish, no less in their religious practice than in any other aspect of their lives. I find the following anecdote of particular interest. In his memoirs, Arthur O'Neill, the blind musician, recounts an incident relating to Christmas 1750 or thereabouts. Arriving at Navan, Co. Meath, he met one Thady Elliot, a fellow harpist who might be described as the resident musician at the little chapel of the Catholic community. O'Neill himself takes up the story:

> On a Christmas Day, Thady was to play at the Roman Catholic chapel of Navan, and a humorous fellow in Navan took Thady to a

public house and promised to give him a gallon of whiskey if he rattled up "Planxty Connor" at the time of the Elevation, which Thady promised to do. Accordingly when Mass commenced on Christmas morning Thady as usual played some sacred airs until the Elevation, and for the sake of the whiskey and to be as good as his word he lilted up "Planxty Connor". The priest, who was a good judge of music, knew the tune but at that solemn stage of the ceremony he could not speak to Thady. But to show his disapprobation he stamped violently on the altar – so much so that the people exclaimed in Irish, "Dar Dhia, tá an sagart a' damhsa!" that is, "By God, the priest is dancing!" However, after playing "Planxty [Connor]" for some short time he resumed his usual tunes. But when Mass was over Thady was severely reproved and dismissed.[57]

What intrigues me about this story is not the humour, nor the summary dismissal, nor the playing of Planxty at the Elevation – which may be Thady Elliot's only claim to immortal memory – but the attitude of the congregation. They seem to have accepted the notion that the priest's most appropriate response to the dance-music – even at the Elevation – was to dance. It seemed "right" and is therefore a fine illustration of that Celtic trait pointed out by Carmichael: "unable to see and careless to know where the secular began and the religious ended".[58]

The really important fact about the age of persecution is that the faith survived. There was little in the way of development, except for the blossoming of popular prayers and the inculcation of fidelity to the faith, a fidelity which by now had become largely linked with fidelity to fatherland. Both were under severe pressure and strain: survival itself was a triumph. When Padraic Colum, the modern Irish poet, stood gazing at the Irish college in Paris and later penned his thoughts, it was that spirit of survival which struck him more than anything else:[59]

> Our order broken, they who were our brood
> Knew not themselves the heirs of noted masters,
> Of Columbanus and Erigena.
>
> We strove towards no high reach of speculation
> Towards no delivery of gestated dogma
> No resolution of age-long disputes.
>
> Only to have a priest beside the hedges,
> Baptising, marrying,
> Offering Mass within some clod-built chapel,
> And to the dying the last sacraments
> Conveying; no more we strove to do –
> We are bare exiles, soldiers, scholars, priests.

5 "Le catholicisme du type irlandais"

The fusion of the terms "Irish" and "Catholic" which came about during
the persecution gave Irish Catholicism a mystique which tended to dis-
engage it from a broad historical context.[1] To quote Desmond Fennell,
one of our more thoughtful men of letters: "it was assumed *a priori*,
by themselves (the Irish) and others, that they were not primarily
human beings involved in modern Anglo-Saxon culture and late Tridentine Catholicism but primarily, in an over-riding sort of way, 'Irish
Catholics', – which could mean whatever you wanted it to mean".[2]
It is unfortunate, too, that of all the fifteen hundred years of Christianity
in Ireland, its "public image", so to speak, should have been taken from
the nineteenth century, which in many ways was probably the least
"Irish" and indeed, the least "Catholic".

In this chapter, I shall outline briefly some of the key factors involved
in the making of modern Irish Catholicism – a phenomenon which some
Continental commentators refer to as "le catholicisme du type irlandais". (the Irish brand of Catholicism).[3] Later in the chapter I shall
treat of some aspects of traditional Catholicism which survived side by
side with the "type irlandais".

Crucial to an understanding of Irish Catholicism from the late eighteenth century to the mid-twentieth are three factors:
(a) The cultural influence of Anglo-Saxon Puritanism;
(b) The large-scale importation of spiritualities;
(c) The centralisation and "Romanisation" of the Church in Ireland.

(a) The cultural influence of Anglo-Saxon Puritanism

Whether through a spirit of loyalty or a recognition of the status quo,
the Irish people in general, whether old Gaelic or foreign settlers, recognised the overlordship of the English king from the Norman invasion
onwards. There were rebellions indeed, especially during the Tudor reign
of terror, but in the seventeenth century Irish Catholics supported
Charles I, and later fought for James II, continuing to give loyalty to
the exiled Stuarts until the second half of the eighteenth century.

But, as the eighteenth century progressed, significant developments
took place in Ireland. Outright persecution declined but the Catholic
population was still discriminated against, being debarred from holding
government office or entering parliament. A host of lesser restrictions
also remained on the statute book. The situation for Catholics was

further complicated by the fact that the papacy continued to acknow-
ledge the Stuarts as the legitimate rulers of England and recognised their
privileges regarding the appointment of bishops in Ireland. However, the
papacy refrained from acknowledging the claims of Charles III (Bonnie
Prince Charlie), thus effectively creating in Ireland a separation of Church
and State (as far as the Catholic Church was concerned) dating from
1761. This new situation paved the way for acceptance of the Hanoverian
line in the person of George III who acceded to the throne in that year.
In fact, an emerging middle-class Irish Catholic community developed
an obsequious loyalty to the British Crown.

The depths to which this class descended may be gleaned from the
"Address of the Roman Catholick Noblemen and Gentlemen of the
Counties of Meath and Westmeath" which appeared in the *London
Gazette,* 3 February 1761, on the occasion of the accession of George.
The memorialists begin by humbly presuming

> to join in our most affectionate and sincere Affliction to your
> Majesty's Tears, for the much-lamented Death of your Royal Grand-
> father; a Death universally deplored by all your mourning Subjects,
> but not by any, more deeply, or more justly felt, than by your
> poor and distressed Roman Catholicks . . . who bear in their Breasts,
> Monuments of eternal Gratitude, for the Indulgence, Favour and
> Clemency, which he and his Royal Father were most graciously
> pleased to extend to them on several Occasions.[4]

What those occasions were, the noble and gentlemanly memorialists
do not specify, but go on undaunted:

> And now we raise our flowing Eyes, from the Obsequies of our late
> good and merciful King, to your Majesty's Throne; where, with un-
> speakable and heart-felt Joy, we behold all his shining Virtues in
> your Majesty's Royal Person as hereditary as his Crown.[5]

"It was of the same royal grandfather", says historian John Brady —
with appropriate smile I imagine — "that Thackery wrote a century later:
'here was one who had neither dignity, learning, morals, nor wit — who
tainted a great society by a bad example; who, in youth, manhood, old
age, was gross, low and sensual'."[6] Well could Daniel O'Connell, The
Liberator, prophesy: "In times to come people will not give me due
credit for the winning of Catholic Emancipation, for it will not enter
into the mind of man to conceive of what race of slaves I have to endeavour to make men."[7]

There was more to the above-mentioned address than the sonorous
language of the obsequious memorialists. It was the voice of a new
breed, a Catholic merchant and propertied class who felt that there was
a future for them in Ireland if they would but accept the language and
tradition of their masters. The language was English. The tradition was

neither Irish nor Catholic, but an Anglo-Saxon puritanical culture which
had come to pervade not only English society, but that of America and
indeed of the entire English-speaking world.

On the nature and values enshrined in this culture now embraced
by the Catholic middle class in Ireland, Desmond Fennell comments:

> The mid-nineteenth century Liberal writer, John Stuart Mill saw
> "the two influences which have chiefly shaped the British character
> since the days of the Stuarts" as commercial money-getting business
> and Religious Puritanism". Besides "commercial" and "puritanical" a
> full characterisation of the predominant cultural stream in nine-
> teenth century Britain, America, and Australia would have to in-
> clude: democratic, liberal-utilitarian, anti-intellectual, philistine, iso-
> lationist in regard to continental European culture.[8]

When the Catholic Church in England collapsed like a house of cards
at the Reformation, the Catholic tradition was soon replaced by puritanical culture. No such collapse took place in Ireland. But with the
political destruction of the nation and the decline of the language, a
whole people was cut adrift from fourteen hundred years of Christian
tradition and over two thousand years of native language and custom.
They were left, therefore, without any adequate mode of expression
culturally familiar to them.

The growing sense of freedom in the late eighteenth and early nineteenth centuries found the Catholics of Ireland without culture, custom,
or language in which to express the ancient faith. A new brand of
Catholicism emerged on the Irish scene — an ancient Catholic creed
expressing itself in the context of an Anglo-Saxon puritanical Protestant
culture. Small wonder that it produced something of a bastard religion,
a Catholic-Protestantism which, even to this day, cannot be categorised
by the ordered Continental mind and is, therefore, set aside in a special
category all to itself under "le catholicisme du type irlandais". Not
classifying it with the European brand of Catholicism was, perhaps,
justifiable, but as Mr Fennell points out: "It was not its 'Irishness' that
was at stake but the centuries-old contact with Anglo-Saxon culture,
which in the nineteenth century became an immersion. It was by
adopting the English language, important elements of English political
practice and of English civil and middle-class morality, that the Irish
produced a Catholicism which was European in its roots and yet trans-
cended Europe."[9]

In the question of sexual mores, for example, the Irish tradition
had been exceedingly well-balanced until the advent of the Puritans.
Indeed, some views on the matter might be considered overly liberal,
a case in point being the eulogising of Cathal Óg MacManus Maguire in
the *Annals of Ulster*. Cathal Óg, a priest and father of over a dozen illegitimate children, is lauded by the annalist not merely for his high offices,

hospitality and scholarly attainment — that, we can readily endorse — but also as a gem of purity and a turtle dove of chastity.[10]

Again, the marriage-shy Irish syndrome, a phenomenon of the late nineteenth and early twentieth centuries, can scarcely be attributed to the "Irishness" in the culture. Rather the reverse, if we bear in mind that:

(a) in the mid-eighteenth century, Dr Madgett, in his *Constitutiones Ecclesiasticae*, notes that "girls often marry around or before their twenty-first year";

(b) that the census figures for the early nineteenth century show a marked tendency towards early marriage among the people;[12]

(c) that Protestants in Ireland have a marriage rate which is lower and later than that of Catholics;[13]

(d) that in the late nineteenth century, the narrow restricting views of Continental European moral theologians came to be applied and enforced in a manner never known on this island.

Perhaps at this point a reference to another matter concerning culture and religion might not be out of place. I refer to the oft-quoted term "Irish Jansenism". That there was some Jansenism in Ireland is scarcely to be doubted,[14] but Jansenism, like Gallicanism, became a vague term meaning at times little more than a certain austerity, and austerity has always been a hall-mark of traditional Irish piety. The term "Irish Jansenism" is misleading. More often than not "Anglo-Saxon Puritanism" is the relevant expression.

(b) The large-scale importation of spiritualities

In the eighteenth century, a format of prayer and brand of piety was developing which would remain with us down to Vatican II. Catholic in theology, it was disseminated through the medium of English against a backdrop of the all-pervading Anglo-Saxon puritanical culture.

For an account of this development it is hard to improve on a brief but learned article by Tomás Uasal de Bhál:[15]

With the publication of Archbishop James Butler's catechism in 1777, religion had acquired the idiom which is still current: the language of prayer had been formulated, and many religious exercises had taken definite shape . . . Primate O'Reilly's catechism preceded Butler's and held its own ground in Ulster; but Butler's gradually became the standard formulary of Catholic belief and practice for all Ireland and for much of the English-speaking world — at the third plenary Council of Baltimore many of the Fathers were in favour of making Butler the official compendium of Christian doctrine for the United States . . .

Butler, the second James of his name to be Archbishop of Cashel, was a young man, thirty-five years of age, in 1777, and lived in a thatched house in Thurles. His contemporaries in the metropolitan centres — Challoner in London, Hay in Edinburgh and Carpenter in Dublin — were older and had already done and were still to do much towards establishing a uniform pattern of prayer and devotion. They were not remiss in posting the paths to paradise, laying down and planting gardens of the soul, and providing prototypes of those keys to heaven which have not yet gone out of use.

The influence of Richard Challoner was supreme. As translator of the Bible he gave our religious literature its peculiar rhythm and cadence. He supplied us with a whole library of spirituality, as popular in Ireland as it was in his own country. His "Garden of the Soul", first published in 1740, was the ancestor of all our prayer-books. Its subtitle defined its scope: "a manual of sacred exercises and instructions for Christians who, living in the world, aspire to devotion". It contained many of the prayers still current (and ceremonies that have not since changed,[16] e.g. the ceremony of Benediction of the Blessed Sacrament, are in the "Garden" described for the first time in the English language. It superseded the older and more liturgical prayer-books, the "Primer" and the "Manual". Much as Challoner himself loved these, they were now relegated to the upper classes while the "Garden" came to terms with the common man, the townsman more perhaps than the countryman, and that was important in the late eighteenth century when a Catholic middle class began to emerge in the cities and towns of Ireland.[17]

"Only less than that of Challoner was the influence of George Hay, vicar-apostolic of the Lowland district of Scotland, in shaping the pattern of prayer and devotion of Irish Catholics of his time."[18] Hay's publications — *Sincere Christian, Devout Christian, Pious Christian*, etc. — were immensely popular in Ireland. His works enjoyed support from the Irish bishops, especially those of the Leinster province. Thus began the wholesale importation of Catholic piety into Ireland.

A good part of the success of British religious publications in Ireland was due to lack of competition from the Irish side. It was not that the Irish lacked spirituality. They lacked language to express it. English, the new medium, could neither express in depth or accuracy the Gaelic approach to God. The Irish language and culture had become thoroughly imbued with Christian and Catholic sentiment, whereas, in an oft-quoted phrase of an old Cork Capuchin, "the English language is the language of heresy". In the nineteenth-century Irish scene it certainly was. The problem was not the English language itself but the culture which was inseparable from it.

However, despite the good Capuchin's assertion, it must be stated clearly that the language of the towns had always been English and the towns, with the exception of Carrickfergus, remained staunchly loyal to the Catholic faith and developed a piety which was adequate.

It must also be borne in mind that the towns never integrated with the Gaelic culture. The bishops in the late eighteenth and early nineteenth centuries were confronted with a difficult choice — should Irish or English be chosen as the medium for handing on the faith. On the one hand, the traditional vehicle, Irish language and culture, was in decline, while English, the language of the newly emerging merchant class in the towns, and the language of an expanding empire, had the tide in its favour. Most of the bishops sailed with that tide, though not always without feelings of perplexity.

John Carpenter, the Archbishop of Dublin, an able scholar and lover of the Gaelic language, published a "Rituale" in 1776 containing instructions on religious matters in simple Irish. But, faced with the problem of governing a traditionally English-speaking diocese and seeing such an output of spiritual writing in that language, he seems to have lost heart or judged it better to let the move towards English take its course.

But Britain wasn't the only source of new spirituality for the Irish. The Continent, itself in a valley period as far as spirituality goes, was an equally prominent source. From France, Belgium, Italy and elsewhere poured in new approaches, new ideas, new religious orders and groupings of one kind or another, each with its own brand of piety and accompanying badge, medal or holy chord. Spiritual nosegays and particular *examens*, Francis de Sales and Père Grou, processions and sparkling shrines: all began to figure largely in the Irish spiritual diet, as did jubilees, tridua, novenas, missions, Forty Hours, perpetual adoration, blessed altars, Benediction, stations of the cross, devotions to the Sacred Heart and to the Immaculate Conception, confraternaties, sodalities of everything and anything and nothing, societies of many brands — Vincent de Paul, temperance, purgatorian. A host of back-up services also existed, providing scapulars, missals, prayer-books, medals, holy pictures, Agnus Dei, prayers that never fail to be answered, and, of course — something already familar and loved — the rosary-beads.

Now there's nothing very wrong with much of the above; indeed a great deal of good has been derived from it, but its greatest weakness, to my mind, is that it did not appreciate or take account of the people and the tradition. For a summary comment on the switch from the old piety to the new, I return to Tomás de Bhál:

> So it comes that down to our own time our piety has been of the eighteenth century, Georgian in style and pattern rather than Gothic or Gaelic; our formal praying has been, so to speak, a kind of period-piece, more suited to the squares and broad streets of Dublin than to the Irish countryside . . .
>
> One is loth to be critical of so venerable a corpus of prayer and piety but may one most respectfully suggest that it may be too sustained where it should be a little more spontaneous, too civilised and

urban where it should be a bit bedraggled and daring and rural, too
elaborate where it should be inspired, too flat and level when it
should be soaring to the skies, too articulate and too fully stated for
the Celtic mentality for which, as Kuno Meyer said, the "half-said
thing is dearest".[19]

(c) The centralisation and "Romanisation" of the Church in Ireland
   That the Church in Ireland needed some special attention and reform
after the chaotic era of persecution goes without saying. The faith itself
was strong but there were weaknesses in structure and discipline. With
the advent of Catholic Emancipation in 1829, the Church was free to
devote itself to reorganising the restructuring. In the words of Desmond
Fennell:

> The new Irish church was almost totally unencumbered by dead
> baggage or by mortgages from the past and was very poor, materially
> and culturally. There was not even an "ancien régime" in the back-
> ground for reactionaries to hark back to or for progressives to use as
> a bogeyman. Modern Irish Catholicism had the freedom and strength
> which youth and poverty offer. Because it was rich in faith it was
> able to use them.[20]

   Rich in faith it was. The strong-arm tactics of the days of persecution
yielded a poor harvest to the so-called Reformed Church. There were
those after Emancipation who believed that the velvet glove could succeed where force had failed. Thus, in the mid-nineteenth century, the
country was subjected to an onslaught from Anglican zealots who,
taking advantage of the poverty and famine in the land, roamed the
country from end to end with "a Bible in one hand and a soup ticket
in the other".[21] Yet the census of 1861 revealed that their effort was
largely futile.[22]
   Among the clergy there was still much pettiness and squabbling; and
dissension was prevalent among the hierarchy, particularly on the vexed
question regarding what stand it should take *vis-à-vis* the British government's educational policies for Ireland. In October 1851, Michael Jones,
a former student of Propaganda's Urban College in Rome, complained
to Cardinal Franzoni: "The Irish people are very good, but much
neglected in every way by both the Civil and Ecclesiastical Government,
more by the latter than the former."[23] Jones might have done well to
withold his complaint, because the previous year, 1850, had seen two
events which were to transform the face of Irish Catholicism. The first
of these events was the appointment of Paul Cullen to the vacant pri-
matial see of Armagh; the second was the National Synod of Thurles —
the first of its kind in Ireland since the twelfth century.
   Dr Cullen had spent thirty years in Rome as a student, professor in

Propaganda College, vice-rector of the Irish College, Roman Procurator of the Irish and Australian Bishops, and, in 1849, *rector pro tempore* of Propaganda College. He was well aware of the Irish scene and shared the anxiety of the Holy See over the disunity that was evident among the Irish hierarchy. His standing among the Roman authorities was such that his advice was sought, not only on Irish affairs but on many other matters as well.

A man who had "become imbued with the current Roman out-look",[24] Cullen comes across to us as a devoted bishop, anxious only to promote the welfare of the Catholic Church; a tireless champion of the poor, a very able organiser and administrator, and an advocate of strict ecclesiastical discipline. Always a firm opponent of political violence, he nevertheless took a strictly independent attitude to government and civic administration. He regarded the role of bishops and priests as one of spiritual service and duties towards their flocks and strongly empha-sised the value of ecclesiastical obedience of priests to bishops and of bishops to the Pope. He ensured that the instructions and decisions of Propaganda were based on the fullest knowledge of the Irish situation and he then set himself to carry out the policy of the Holy See as faith-fully as possible.[25]

The Synod of Thurles, the second event marking out 1850 as a turn-ing point in the history of the Irish Church, sat between 22 August and 10 September. The scope of its activity was wideranging, as indicated by its one hundred and eighty-nine decrees on eleven separate topics: faith, sacraments (with the exception of holy orders), life of the clergy, parish priest, curate, bishop, keeping of archives, Church property, education (two sections), and clerical dissensions.[26] Present in his dual capacity as leader of the Irish hierarchy and apostolic delegate of Pius IX, Dr Cullen hoped that the synod would "lay the foundation of a good and general system of Canon Law for the Irish Church",[27] and on this foundation he was to strive for the rest of his life to build an organised and disciplined Church, governed by a united and disciplined hierarchy.

Cullen's success as a reformer was in no small measure due to his very considerable personal skills as an ecclesiastical politician, plus the strong support of Rome, especially in the matter of episcopal appointments. Referring to the kind of candidates put forward by Cullen for filling episcopal sees in Ireland, Emmet Larkin says:

> In general Cullen preferred to promote men . . . who were made in his own image and likeness. They were not only good preachers, adequate theologians, zealous, courageous enough, and young, but they were also generally strangers to the diocese and, therefore, they did not have any of the personal ties or loyalties that might inhibit them in their zeal for reform. If they were not recruited from the regular clergy, moreover, the new bishops were usually rectors or

vice-rectors of seminaries — strict, stern, austere men who had both the experience of, and a proven talent for, effective administration. They were also well aware that the new discipline they represented would not be popular among their priests, but if these bishops were ever to make their wills effective with their clergy, the bishops would have to depend on their patron's continued exertions on their behalf at Rome. They all tended, therefore, to be ultramontanes because Rome was not only the theoretical but the actual source of their own and Cullen's real power in the Irish Church.[28]

Among the many problems needing urgent attention were clerical avarice and the administering of sacraments in private houses. Both of these problems died hard. Indeed, if the truth were told, they did not die at all: the former has always lurked in the background while the latter has taken on a new air of dignity, respectability and universality in the post-Vatican II Church.

In the eyes of the bishops the main clerical vices were wine, women and avarice. Lust and drunkenness, especially the latter, might be tolerated by the people as weakness, but, in the words of Bishop Moriarty of Kerry, "avarice they never pardon either in life or death; it is for them as the sin against the Holy Ghost — quod non remittetur, neque in hoc saeculo, neque in futuro (Matt 12:32)" [who shall not be forgiven neither in this world nor in the world to come (Matt 12:32)].[29] Moriarty further reminds his clergy: "no amount of piety, no integrity of life, no seeming zeal, no labour in the work of the priesthood, will gain for an avaricious man the goodwill of the people".[30]

As always in the face of problems that refuse to go away, the people resorted to the usual palliatives of humour and satire. The language and lore of the nation abound with tales of clerical greed. The eighteenth-century poet, Owen Roe O'Sullivan, poses himself the question: "When will the raven talk?" and in reply says:

> Nuair a thiocfaidh an míol-mór ar an Maing,
> Nuair a thiocfaidh an Fhrainc go Sliabh Mís,
> Nuair a chaillfidh an sagart a' t-saint,
> Ansan a thiocfaidh an caint do'n bhfiachdubh.

> (When the whale comes up the River Main,
> When France comes to Slieve Mish,
> When the priest loses his greed,
> Then will the raven talk.)

Associated with the problem of avarice was the custom of celebrating the sacraments of baptism, eucharist, penance and matrimony in private houses. While the custom probably had its origins in the exigencies of penal days, it was alleged that its continuation was for a less worthy motive, the financial remuneration accruing to the clergy.[31]

When the National Synod of Thurles addressed itself to the reform of Irish Church practice, it paid particular attention to the question of celebrating sacraments in private houses; the pastoral custom of holding "stations" bore the brunt of the attack.

Stations, which originated in the penal days or earlier, was a practice well-suited to an Irish tradition of intimate communities. A parish was divided into "station areas" and every spring and autumn, the priests (the pastor and an assistant usually) visited every station area where, in a designated house chosen on a basis of rotation, the priests heard confessions, celebrated Mass and distributed Holy Communion. The stations were a godsend to the people, especially the feeble and the elderly who had little chance of walking four, eight, or more miles over very rough terrain to the nearest church.

Complaints were made about the wretchedness of the houses where the Holy Mass was celebrated,[32] and about the financial outlay and the priest's attitude in this regard,[33] but the real stumbling-block as far as Rome was concerned was the custom of hearing women's confessions "extra sedem confessionalem" (outside of the place for confession).[34] It seems that many Continentals, and those Irish churchmen imbued with the Roman spirit, could scarcely envisage a priest being alone with a woman without sin on the part of either or both. Cullen would settle for nothing less than the abolition of hearing women's confessions outside of the confessional, as is evident from his rejection of the mild decree passed by the Synod of Thurles.[35] He pointed out to Propaganda that hearing confessions of women in private houses was "pieno di pericoli per i sacerdoti, specialmente giovani" (full of dangers for priests, especially young priests).[36] Cullen's uncle, Fr Maher, had no doubts about the problem: "The young clergyman is brought in contact with his female penitents. The result is confessions are often invalid or sacrilegious."[37]

Stations were finally outlawed by Rome, but persisted in several Irish dioceses — especially in the south and west. Their survival is, I think, a healthy sign, a triumph of the spirit over the law, for they were good pastoral practice not merely "peccatores reconciliantes et panem vitae distribuentes" (reconciling sinners and distributing the bread of life) but also "scandala si quae sint removentes, dissentiones componentes, amicitiam et charitatem cum omnibus colentes, consiliariorum munere fungentes" (eliminating any scandals they come across, healing · dissensions, cultivating friendship and charity with all, and exercising the role of counsellors).[38]

At a popular and devotional level the renewal of the faith was gaining ground. A "devotional revolution"[39] was under way, and this contributed further to the Romanisation and Continentalisation of the Irish Church. At the end of the 1830s a young Capuchin friar, Theobald Matthew, threw in his lot with the advocates of temperance in the use of alcohol and, mainly through his zeal and dedicated preaching, the consumption of whiskey fell by more than half, and that within five years (1839-44).[40]

To a variety of jubilees and missions the people responded with the most marvellous displays of faith and enthusiasm. Of the Carlow mission in 1843, an eyewitness declared: "Hundreds remained all night in the chapel, and many remained in town away from their homes for five and six days waiting an opportunity for confessing."[41] Of the same mission, Paul Cullen's sister, Margaret, wrote to him that it "would be impossible for me to describe the enthusiasm of the people. If the missioners were angels from heaven, they could not be more venerated." She described how work was at a standstill, while people followed the missioners around all day and crowded "in hundreds to the Confessionals, many, very many who had never before been there". The missioners preached three times a day in the chapel, which was "crowded to suffocation". "What a pity", she finally concluded, "we have not more priests in the parish."[42]

Nine years later, Cullen, now Archbishop of Dublin, wrote to Fr Kirby (his successor in the Irish College): "Here we are trying to enrol a large missionary body before next Summer to wipe out the proselytisers everywhere . . . The Jesuits, Dominicans, Carmelites, Vincentians, Redemptorists, secular Priests will all join together."[43]

The work of popular renewal continued and the people flocked to missions and devotions, whether preached by men with a French, Italian, Belgian, British, Dutch or Russian background. The people were moulded into a thoroughly sacramental and Mass-going Church. In half a century or so[44] the Mass attendance increased from an estimated 30-40 per cent to over 90 per cent and "the great mass of the Irish people became practising Catholics, which they have uniquely and essentially remained both at home and abroad down to the present day".[45]

The whole progress of the nineteenth century in Ireland, with its renewal of Church structures, training of clergy, building of churches, expansion of religious life, and devotional revolution, might well be seen as one triumphal march. But the truth, to my mind, is less flattering. Success there was beyond doubt. But the progress was not so much earned as gained in a somewhat dishonest manner. At best it was a display of big spending on the part of somebody who had received a legacy. What I mean is this: the nineteenth century apostles of the Church achieved their aims in Ireland, not necessarily because of their personal worth or the message they had to offer, but because of the vast reserves of faith in the hearts of the people. At the same time, these nineteenth-century churchmen virtually ignored, and sometimes openly opposed, what were in fact the very sources of that faith, namely, fourteen centuries of unbroken and life-giving Christian tradition passed on in the erstwhile vernacular – Irish – and the tradition which it embodied.

When "le catholicisme du type irlandais" became the new religion of Ireland towards the end of the nineteenth century there was bitter disappointment in the heart of many a cleric and layman who was sharp enough to realise what was really happening. Fr Walter Conway of Glenamaddy, Co. Galway, verbalised his disappointment at the supplanting of a tradition:

> The prayers and the Religious Poems which our ancestors composed and used to repeat, have been given up . . . pieces which came from the heart of him who composed them, and which went straight from the heart of him who said them to the ear of God. And what have we in their place? Ráiméis (i.e. nonsense) which half of those who repeat it do not understand, and from which they reap neither fruit nor profit.[46]

"Le catholicisme du type irlandais" as a phenomenon of the late Tridentine era may well be drawing to a close. A decline seems inevitable; but in that decline we may rediscover a more enduring link with the tradition of Irish spirituality. I often wonder if Austin Clarke is not grappling with this very point in "Emancipation":[47]

> That wretched girl still wakes me up
> At night, for all she wore had been thrown
> Away. I see her by O'Connell Bridge
> And think: "Yes, more than a century
> Ago, religion went in such rags here."
> But pity is a kind of lust,
> Although it stretch and turn. Have I
> Not found at last what covers mine,
> In the cast-off finery of faith?

6 "A list of doors that truth had left unlatched"

Despite the slide towards English in language and culture over the past two centuries, many elements of the old Gaelic tradition continued and still continue to assert themselves. In such a work as this, one must be content with impressionistic images, but from them it will be sufficiently clear that all is not lost. There is, in the words of Patrick Kavanagh, "A list of doors that truth had left unlatched".[1]

These unlatched doors are not for the atavist, nor for the romantic; rather are they gifts to those whose sensitivity to the past guides them towards the evolution of a more authentic and living expression of the Christian faith in the Ireland of today and the Ireland of tomorrow.

In October 1790, a Frenchman, Charles Etienne Coquebert de Montbret, paid a visit to Kerry and the south-west. Coquebert was no ordinary tourist, but a brilliant scholar and an experienced investigator. An edited version of his diary now available makes very interesting reading.[2] Coquebert is convinced that the Catholic religion, "a religion that encourages politeness and lenience",[3] plays a big part in forming the character of the people:

> The goodness of these people reveals itself in their love of children and in their kindness to strangers. When they give charity they do so with an air of politeness to avoid humiliating the recipient, and the best place at the fire is reserved for the poor man. They are full of imagination and quick to understand what one wants to know. If they lack the required information, they straight away invent a story to provide an answer, where in a similar case a German would just keep on saying ich weiss nicht, ich weiss nicht, ten times.[4]

A beautiful illustration of this inventiveness is related of a Kerry priest in the nineteenth century who, in his pastoral visitation during the Great Famine, consoled the living and buried the dead with dignity. Speaking to a woman who had lost her twin boys — boys well-loved by the old priest — he tried to hold back the tears as he spoke words of comfort to the distraught mother:

> You see, Máire, God wanted the pair, and the high angel, Michael, marked them to fill two grand places and to prepare places for you and their father who is working down in Limerick. There they are this minute, Donnchadh O'Shea [the departed piper] playing "Bó na leath-adhairce" for them, and the Glorious Maiden herself bringing

them around, one by each hand, to meet the old neighbours, all talking about the Regatta at the Pattern and the fine rowing of the Fearanniarach boys. And they must also help the thrushes to build their nests there, and tumble about with the young hares. You mustn't be weeping, Máire.

"I see the tears running down your own face Father", replied the mother, but the kindly priest continued to hide his own grief: "It's only the mountain mist, only the mountain mist, Máire."[5]

The French traveller goes on to compare the Irish and the English:

The native Irish are very different from the people of England. When an Englishman grows wealthy he has no desire to expend money in proportion to his increased wealth. From peer to shopkeeper the English all live in almost the same way — snug and comfortable. But in Ireland as in France every man increases his expenditure in proportion to his profits. The Irish are also more friendly than the English and are far more anxious to acquire knowledge. The people of Munster have a passionate desire for learning and spare nothing to give their children the best possible education, according to their means. Formerly every fairly well-to-do family kept a Latin master in its house and all the children in the neighbourhood were taught by him.[6]

A contemporary of Coquebert, Arthur Young — an Englishman — did a tour of Ireland about the same time and was struck by the "vivacity and a great and eloquent volubility of speech . . . They are infinitely more cheerful and lovely than anything we commonly see in England, having nothing of that incivility of sullen silence, with which so many enlightened Englishmen seem to wrap themselves up, as if retiring within their own importance."[7] Arthur Young, though not as reliable as Coquebert,[8] has no difficulty in expounding some further qualities of the Irish, who are

so spiritedly active at play, that, at hurling, which is the cricket of savages, they show the greatest feats of agility. Their love for society is as remarkable as their curiosity is insatiable; and their hospitality to all comers, be their own poverty ever so pinching, has too much merit to be forgotten. Pleased to enjoyment with a joke, or witty repartee, they will repeat it with such expression, that the laugh will be universal . . . dancing is so universal among them that there are everywhere itinerant dancing masters, to whom the cottars pay sixpence a quarter for teaching their families.[9]

Irish hospitality extends no less to the dead than to the living. Whether or not this bond with the departed antedates Christianity, I shall not explore here. Suffice it to say that it is still with us and has always been characteristic of our religious expression. There was a widespread belief, for instance, that the dead members of the family visisted their old home at the beginning of November, the ancient pagan Irish feast of "Samhain" which fitted in so admirably with "All Saints" and "All Souls" in the Christian calendar. Leaving the lock off the door, having a good fire in the hearth, and placing a bowl of water on the table was a common mode of preparing the house for a possible visit from the dead. So too was the custom of lighting a candle for each dead member – a ritual performed during evening prayer in the home. Kevin Danaher, the folklorist, once asked an old man if he were not afraid to enter a haunted house. "In dread of it?" replied the old man, "What would I be in dread of, and the souls of my own dead as thick as bees around me."[10] Having offered Mass at home on Samhain Night (1976) I said to my aged father: "They were all there tonight." "They were", he replied with perfect understanding, as if I had been referring to a congregation of the living, but at that Mass the only visible persons present were himself and one of my sisters. Whether people were "alive" or "dead" made little difference to him, for he was of a tradition that drew no hard and fast lines between life in "gleann na ndeoir" (vale of tears) or "Tír na nÓg" (Land of Youth – Heaven).

One of the loveliest descriptions of a family at prayer on All Souls Night, comes from a Co. Limerick farm-house in the late nineteenth century. It was the one night in the year on which the rosary was not said. There was a special ritual for that night:

> ... father drew his chair and mother's into the middle of the kitchen, for this was the one night of the year when we did not say the Rosary; we children moved near to them and Dinny-bawn sat on the floor at father's feet; the servants drew out the forms and knelt against them with the fiddler and Murnane. When the shuffling of feet quietened and the room was still, father read the litany of the Dead: very solemn and lonely it was. We made the responses in hushed voices as if we were listening for the rustling of home-faring souls. Father prayed for his own dead and for mother's by name ... "my father, Michael, Thy Servant ... Mammy Mac and Mammy Jug, Thy Servants, Catherine and Joanna"; for "the lord" and other departed friends. He did not forget Ellie's and Bridgie's parents, nor Murnane's wife. He prayed for "Dick Dooley, my faithful friend and helper", and for Tom Hickey's father, and for those whom the wandering fiddler had loved and lost. Last of all he prayed for Dinny-bawn's Mary:
>
> > Eternal rest grant to them, O Lord,
> > And may perpetual light shine upon them.[11]

Liturgical changes in the nineteen-sixties – temporarily I expect – dampened the celebration of the feast of Samhain, at least that aspect of it which pays special honour to the dead. Admittedly, the plenary indulgence for every six paters, aves and glorias wasn't an ideal approach to "liberating Holy Souls", but there was a certain atmosphere, tradition, ethos, which has to be re-established. The fact that in the town cemetery at Tuam, Co. Galway, on 2 November 1976, a most impressive gathering of men, women and children congregated for Mass for their dead, despite very inclement weather, is an indication that rebuilding this tradition, at least, will not be a difficult undertaking.

Pilgrimage is another expression of the faith of the people which has survived the nineteenth century and is now regaining much of its popularity. The pilgrimage phenomenon has always been quite extraordinary, and a high percentage of modern Irish have been on pilgrimage of one kind or another either at home or overseas.

The most popular shrines and pilgrim-centres at home are Knock, Croagh Patrick and Lough Derg. Though less frequented, still popular are Faughart, Glendalough, Lady's Island, Ballyvourney, Clonmacnoise, and Ballyheigue, among others. The pattern of pilgrimage to foreign parts has changed somewhat. No longer included in the general run of foreign pilgrimages are Compostella or Iona, but still very popular are Rome, the Holy Land, and the more recent European shrines of Fatima and Lourdes. I must add, however, that this listing in no way exhausts the catalogue of shrines frequented each year by Irish pilgrims.

Of the Irish pilgrim-centres, Knock, Co. Mayo, attracts by far the greatest number of pilgrims in any given year. As a place of devotion it is of relatively recent origin. In 1879 the Mother of God and other heavenly personalities are said to have appeared there. Since then it has grown in popularity becoming *the* Marian shrine of the land. Despite the recent erection of a vast new basilica, the windswept landscape around Knock has retained much of its native characteristics, and the warm spirit and faith of the pilgrims is inspiring.

A Romanian priest, Fr John Filip, visiting the shrine in 1956, noted:

> . . . the pilgrim throng that encircled the church quietly reciting the rosary or devoutly kneeling at the oratory of the apparition . . . It is here one comes into direct contact with the very soul of Ireland . . . at Knock one is struck in a special way by the cordiality and warm family-spirit which pervades and with which the invalids are treated and ministered to by the good Handmaids and stewards who fulfil their wonderful apostolate with great faith and a deep spirit of sacrifice.[12]

That his observations are equally true of the Knock of twenty years later I can personally vouch.

Whether or not the Mother of God appeared at Knock is almost an irrelevancy at this stage in history. What is important is that the spot continues to be a power-house of prayer, a centre of community worship for the people of the land, a spot where people with a traditional love for Jesus and his mother can pour their hearts out in prayer with freedom of spirit. Time and again, I have observed groups and individuals of all ages pray at Knock – engaged couples, newly-weds, whole families, multitudes of people from every class and background bound in one set purpose. And how they pray! Heart and soul goes into that pilgrimage: the stations of the cross, the "rounds",[13] the contemplation of the life, death and resurrection of Christ in the fifteen mysteries of the rosary. Finally, the climax of the day, the Eucharist. No fun and games here, no distractions except the almost incessant rain which is viewed with good spirit and incorporated as part of the penitential aspect of the day.

Contrasting the penances involved in making the other two national pilgrimages – Croagh Patrick and Lough Derg – is always a matter for discussion and divergence of views. Personally I have no doubt that Lough Derg is the more difficult, but "personally" is the operative word. It really depends on whether an individual prefers or manages better to survive starvation and sleeplessness over a number of days, or go barefooted up the slopes of a rocky mountain and thus get the most painful part of the pilgrimage over in a matter of perhaps five to seven hours.

Both Lough Derg and Croagh Patrick are Patrician shrines, the national apostle, having, it is said, prayed and fasted forty days and forty nights at each. The former ("St Patrick's Purgatory") is a tiny island shrine in Co. Donegal. The latter, popularly known as "The Reek" from its shape, is a great hulk of quartz dominating the north Connaught horizons and situated in the County of Mayo. The use of the word "mountain" is relative of course. Croagh Patrick is a mere 2,510 feet high; yet, when climbed in bare feet or on one's bare knees, a pilgrim is justly entitled to look upon it as a mountain, and even an Anglo-Saxon or a Dutchman might be forgiven for resorting to hyperbolic terms in describing its magnitude.

To the present day people of all ages climb "The Reek". The pilgrimage may be done at any time of year, but that held on "Reek Sunday" – the last Sunday of July – has a long tradition behind it. Indeed, there is very strong evidence to suggest that the Gaels had resorted to that holy mountain long before St Patrick gave it a Christian orientation.[14] The traditional climb is at night – the dark hours of the vigil so dear to the people – and on that last Sunday in July a vast throng makes the ascent, an estimated twenty thousand on "Reek Sunday" and perhaps up to fifty thousand in the course of a year. Fifty thousand people out of a population of about three million Catholics is a very large number, particularly striking when one considers that the pilgrimage is undertaken without any real support from the institutional Church. There has, in fact, been a degree of discouragement from that quarter, since the vigil Mass at midnight has been prohibited.

I once met a young man on the slopes of that mountain. He was an agnostic from Sweden who had come to immerse himself in the faith of the pilgrims in the hope of finding for himself a new understanding of life. He found it extremely difficult to understand the penitential aspect – the bare feet and the sight of some clinging to the age-old custom of climbing on bare knees. But failure to understand penance is failure to understand Irish Christianity. Suffering with the gentle Christ who suffered for us is integral to the tradition.

As chaplain to a pilgrimage of young people in their late teens or early twenties, I was gaily stepping along the foothills when I noticed that I was virtually the only person who had shoes on. I speedily cast them aside and entered into the spirit as I observed those young men and women joyfully doing penance for themselves and the world about them. It came home to me how I had been so much part of an institution which had distanced itself from the living tradition. For the pilgrims in their penitential climb, there is no encouragement, no compulsion, just simple voluntary choice. As a phenomenon of the last quarter of the twentieth century, such a religious expression has decidedly hopeful possibilities.

For pilgrims to Lough Derg, there is often a journey of five, perhaps even ten, hours by coach and, for some, an overnight stop *en route*. In all, it involves three days – seventy-two hours – fasting. The only concession made to the weakness of the human body is an allowance of black tea and dry toast once a day, with generous, nay, unlimited, quantities of "Lough Derg Soup", which one pilgrim assured me was made from the simple recipe of hot water and pepper.

Before landing on the island, all shoes and stockings must be removed. The sharp loose stones which form the surface of the island provide an excellent opportunity for self-mortification as the pilgrims hobble about making the stations – "stations" in this instance referring to various shrines of Celtic saints. No sleep is allowed all through the first night on the island and, if the preacher's words send the pilgrims peacefully into the arms of Morpheus, there's always a kind friend at hand to ensure that the embrace is not prolonged.

Lough Derg is highly institutionalised, but, underneath, there persists the real surging piety of the people, as thousands come to pray and do penance at "The Purgatory"; some, indeed, return again and again, perhaps as often as twenty or even forty times, though usually at intervals of at least a year.

As to the effects of a pilgrimage to Lough Derg, I can hardly quote better than a conversation I overheard in Dr Pádraig Ó Domhnaill's waiting-room in Dublin on 30 March 1977:

Mrs A: "You'd want to be frightfully fit for it."
Mrs B: "You come out refreshed in mind and heart and body."

Mrs A: "Is it still very rough?"
Miss C: "Yes, and I believe what they say about sharpening the stones
         at night."

   At the provincial and local level, pilgrimages too numerous to mention are made at all times of the year to traditional holy places. At Ballyheigue, for example, there is Kerry's Marian "county shrine". Here,
year by year, on Mary's birthday, 8 September, approximately five
thousand people come to pray. Pilgrims come all year round, but 8 September is the highlight. By long-standing tradition, children are duty-
bound to return on that day and take to the shrine parents or other
relatives who may be unable to make the journey on their own. The
present pastor assured me that this custom is still observed as a most
sacred trust.
   At least twice a year the little town of Ballyvourney in Co. Cork
is thronged to capacity as pilgrims come to the ancient shrine and well
of St Gobnait. Again, as at other wells and shrines, the pilgrims are not
limited to making their visits on those days only. A holy well or shrine
is a spot for prayer at any time; it is a holy place. The Ballyvourney
shrine has been restored in recent years and a limestone statue — executed by the late and much loved Seamus Murphy — dominates the
hallowed spot. The prayer at the base is utterly traditional — simple,
direct, straight from the heart. Mr John J. Lucey, a local shopkeeper,
sent it to me along with many other beautiful prayers still in use among
the people of that district:

> Go mbeannaí Dia dhuit a Ghobnait Naofa,
> Go mbeannaí Muire dhuit is beannaím féin duit.
> Is chughatsa a thánag, ag gearán mo scéil leat,
> Is ag iarraidh me a leigheas ar son Dé ort.
>
> (May God bless you St Gobnait
> May Mary bless you and I greet you myself too.
> It is to you I have come telling you my story,
> And asking you for God's sake to heal me.)

   In the making of an Irish pilgrimage, there are prescribed patterns of
prayer, usually of the repetitive nature so dear to popular piety. The
pilgrimage incorporates many aspects of the Irish tradition. There is the
obvious penitential side associated with most; the notion of repentance,
conversion, prayer for one's own needs, for the Body of Christ — the
universal Church. There is the freedom associated with outdoors and
the closeness to nature: on a mountain, a lake-island, a wooded valley
such as Glendalough or Gougane Barra, both of which, incidentally, have
lakes as well. And, of course, there is the vigil, a religious value and expression dear to Irish spirituality in all ages. Finally, there is that ever-

present peregrinatory passion: it is always sweeter to make a pilgrimage than to say one's prayers at home. Finally, that safety valve of humour is rarely lacking. People from the south-west love to relate how the Bishop of Kerry led his pilgrim people to the top of Mount Brandon to pray and celebrate the Eucharist on the Feast of St Brendan. Brandon Mountain is engulfed in rain and cloud for most of the year. On this particular day the bleak summit was enveloped with biting wind and lashing rain. As the assembled multitude proclaimed the mystery of faith "Christ has died, Christ is risen, Christ will come again", one disenchanted pilgrim was distinctly heard proclaiming: "Christ, I won't come again."

Turning to the penitential proclivity in the Irish approach to God, I believe that much can be gained or lost in the future, depending on the manner in which it is cultivated. Speaking to an aged confrère some time ago, we contrasted in a homely way the difference between Irish and French spirituality. My friend, who has a concrete and colourful approach to language, referred to the tendency on the part of the French towards introspection with their penchant for particular *examens*, and so forth. "It is not natural for the Irishman to take his spiritual temperature," he continued, "but quite natural for him to starve himself, or beat hell out of himself." It was a penetrating comment. The same priest assured me that "fasting like an Irishman" was an expression current on the Continent in the seventeenth century.

Certainly, this penitential element is dear to Irish piety today, not only in conjunction with pilgrimages, but in many other aspects of devotion. In a school retreat which I conducted around 1970, one of the exercises I requested was communal penance: in this case, each young student kneeling on his hands for the duration of five paters, aves, and glorias with the intention of making reparation to Christ for the sins of the world. The students undertook the exercise with generosity, curiosity and a tumult of "ohs" and "ahs". Six years later the teacher in charge informed me that the pupils, now in adulthood, remembered with satisfaction what was for them a very telling religious experience.

Fasting, "starving oneself" as my friend put it, is still a very popular expression of faith, something "natural". After the liturgical reform of the post-Vatican II era, a Co. Cork woman, on being asked to read the lesson on the following Sunday, acceded to the request – but as a "natural" preliminary to reading the word of God, she fasted all day on Saturday. This was typically traditional. Her entire traditional piety came to the fore: what she was undertaking was a very solemn event when she would stand before the people – her people – and proclaim the Word.

Still on the theme of fasting, another very traditional dimension which is alive and strong today is the expression of one's inner convictions and values through the controversial mode of hunger-strike. The hunger-strike in early Christian and pre-Christian times was used, as I have mentioned in Chapter Two, as a means of obtaining redress or strengthening one's bargaining power with God or man. It is still basically that: an assertion of a person's sincerely-held convictions irrespective of an objective assessment of the pros and cons. As I prepared this chapter, twenty men spent over forty days on hunger-strike in one of our high-security prisons, where they are serving sentences for political offences arising out of the troubles in the north of Ireland. The hunger-strike weapon has been used frequently since the outbreak of conflict in the north some years ago. Many have suffered severely and the hearty disapproval of Church and State has pursued some to an early grave. Both of these institutions are wont to lament the negative response to their appeals for generosity and heroism. Has the hunger-strike a message for those who have ears to hear and eyes to see? When young men and women are ready to lay their lives on the line – for whatever cause – the stuff of martyrs is not lacking, even if it may at times be mis-spent.

Equally common with hunger-strike is the custom of fasting for one, two, or three days to draw attention to and raise funds for the Third World.

The personification of the penitential element in Irish spirituality in the present century was a Dublin workman, Matt Talbot, the cause for whose beatification is at an advanced stage. Born in 1856, son of a dock labourer, he became an alcoholic in his early teens and is reputed not to have drawn a sober breath for sixteen years. Sacrificing all to drink, he returned home more than once on his bare feet, having pawned his shoes for drink-money. But extreme though he was in drunkenness, Matt's conversion at the age of twenty-eight was still more astonishing. As one of his fellow-workers put it "he could never go easy on anything".[15] What that little comment meant in practice is revealed in some small way by the following:

Ten hours of every day were now spent on his knees in fervent prayer. He would rise from his plank bed at 2.00 a.m. and pray with outstretched arms till 4.00 a.m. when he prepared himself for his first Mass. If he arrived early, he would kneel outside the Church in all weathers on bare knees (his trouser legs having been slit to admit the penitential cold). After hearing the maximum number of Masses, he completed his devotions with Stations of the Cross and arrived home at 7.00 a.m. for a frugal breakfast of dry bread and a mixture of cold tea and cocoa, taken without milk or sugar. His other meals varied only slightly from the meagre diet. During the last thirteeen years of his life, he wore penitential chains which were only revealed after his death.[16]

Matt's proverbial devotion to the Mass (he heard as many as twenty-

one in the space of two consecutive mornings), his love and devotion
Jesus in the Blessed Sacrament, and his recitation of the fifteen mysteries of the rosary every day, made him one of the greatest exponents
of traditional spirituality the country has ever known. Nor was he lacking in good works. Having paid off all his drinking bills of former years,
his wages went entirely on the service of the poor at home and abroad,
retaining only enough to pay his rent and scant food bill. And far from
being a strike-breaker — as has been stated publicly more than once by
persons who have not studied the facts — Matt was years ahead of his
time in his social outlook.[17]

Before ending my remarks on the penitential aspect of Irish spirituality, I wish to add two love-letters. Daniel O'Connell, the greatest European of his day (though the French may be permitted to place Napoleon
alongside, and the British may like to include that other Irishman,
Wellington) corresponded regularly, daily for a considerable time, with
his wife. Over-burdened though he often was, between his activities at
the House of Commons and his work at the bar — not to speak of the
many other activities which constantly demanded his attention —
O'Connell was strict and traditional in his observance of the Lenten
fast, as the following letters from his wife testify:

Dublin,
April 4th. 1816.

My darling love,

         For your sake I wish next week was over. I really
fear you will starve yourself. The Lent is observed so much more
strictly in Cork than here, but recollect, Darling, you ought to take
care of yourself.[18]

And again, from Dublin, on 8 April:

My dearest love.

      . . . How happy I am to hear from Ellen Connor that
your spirits were so good in Tralee. I am sure, darling, your fasting
and abstinence ought to have kept them down for by what I can learn
you have observed BOTH most strictly. I will venture to say they
were few priests who did more . . .[19]

If the people of Navan, in Co. Meath, saw it fitting for the p
dance at the Consecration of the Mass when Thady Elliot lilted
Connor", so the O'Connell couple in their love letters did oy
thing unusual in addressing themselves to matters of pena

The reform of Church law on fast and abstinen
Pope Paul VI in *Paenitemini* needs careful att
at all sure that we are being successful in makin
a tight system of legal controls to one of perso
ters of self-denial. Since there is a very deep
need to proceed with great sensitivity. Man

...age has been taken out of Christianity, and by "challenge" they simply mean "the penitential element". Though people at large may not have yet grasped the full implications of *Paenitemini*, their instincts are right. In the Celtic world — even more than among any other people perhaps — the "challenge" is needed for the health of the faith.

But the penitential side of life is only one of many areas needing attention and sensitivity. What of all the other constant elements mentioned in Chapter One? The "doors that truth had left unlatched" are all around us if we have but time to ponder and eyes to see. But there is no specific blue-print for renewal of the Irish Church, no handbook, no official guide, no expert, not even a Roman document which gives all the answers. And how thankful we should be for that, for the Church is essentially a believing, worshipping, serving community, and renewal is about tapping the resources of the people, being sensitive to their mode of expressing the faith, interpreting the manifestations of the Holy Spirit. The presence of the Holy Spirit is not always immediately obvious. It may be in Gerry, careless as to sacramental life, but scrupulous in observing Lent as a time of self-denial; it may be in Micheál and Maeve who, accidentally coming upon a group of foreign visitors, took them to their home and "free-gratis-and-for-nothing" treated the strangers to an afternoon of music, song, dance and refreshment before putting them on the train for the next leg of their tour; or it may be in the vigils of the praying multitudes round Mary's shrine in the wind-swept village of Knock in Co. Mayo, or maybe in the heart of a Dublin slum where Christy, touched by the cross of Christ, could tell so vividly of the walk to Calvary in his "Good Friday". Truly, there is a "list of doors that truth had left unlatched", opportunities beyond counting for those who keep faith with the past and face tomorrow with open minds and hearts.

Good Friday

In and out among the narrow little ways of the town
They dragged Him, bearded Man, and the
gems of sweat
On His brow glittered like gold-dust
In the merciless fire of noon-day.
Sticks flashed and thudded dully on straining flesh;
Taunts, maledictions, words sharp
with scorn and hate.
Sank as fire into the tired brain;
Spits bright with foulness ran as lava
down His chest,
the cruel, thin stones of the hillside
...de the blood run from the stumbling Feet,
... the earth with a crimson glory.

one in the space of two consecutive mornings), his love and devotion to Jesus in the Blessed Sacrament, and his recitation of the fifteen mysteries of the rosary every day, made him one of the greatest exponents of traditional spirituality the country has ever known. Nor was he lacking in good works. Having paid off all his drinking bills of former years, his wages went entirely on the service of the poor at home and abroad, retaining only enough to pay his rent and scant food bill. And far from being a strike-breaker — as has been stated publicly more than once by persons who have not studied the facts — Matt was years ahead of his time in his social outlook.[17]

Before ending my remarks on the penitential aspect of Irish spirituality, I wish to add two love-letters. Daniel O'Connell, the greatest European of his day (though the French may be permitted to place Napoleon alongside, and the British may like to include that other Irishman, Wellington) corresponded regularly, daily for a considerable time, with his wife. Over-burdened though he often was, between his activities at the House of Commons and his work at the bar — not to speak of the many other activities which constantly demanded his attention — O'Connell was strict and traditional in his observance of the Lenten fast, as the following letters from his wife testify:

> Dublin,
> My darling love,   April 4th. 1816.
>   For your sake I wish next week was over. I really fear you will starve yourself. The Lent is observed so much more strictly in Cork than here, but recollect, Darling, you ought to take care of yourself.[18]

And again, from Dublin, on 8 April:

> My dearest love,
>   . . . How happy I am to hear from Ellen Connor that your spirits were so good in Tralee. I am sure, darling, your fasting and abstinence ought to have kept them down for by what I can learn you have observed BOTH most strictly. I will venture to say there were few priests who did more . . .[19]

If the people of Navan, in Co. Meath, saw it fitting for the priest to dance at the Consecration of the Mass when Thady Elliot lilted "Planxty Connor", so the O'Connell couple in their love-letters did not see anything unusual in addressing themselves to matters of penance.

The reform of Church law on fast and abstinence as enunciated by Pope Paul VI in *Paenitemini* needs careful attention in Ireland. I am not at all sure that we are being successful in making a sound transition from a tight system of legal controls to one of personal responsibility in matters of self-denial. Since there is a very deep value enshrined here, we need to proceed with great sensitivity. Many people feel that the challenge has been taken out of Christianity, and by "challenge" they simply mean "the penitential element". Though people at large may not have yet grasped the full implications of *Paenitemini,* their instincts are right. In the Celtic world — even more than among any other people perhaps — the "challenge" is needed for the health of the faith.

But the penitential side of life is only one of many areas needing attention and sensitivity. What of all the other constant elements mentioned in Chapter One? The "doors that truth had left unlatched" are all around us if we have but time to ponder and eyes to see. But there is no specific blue-print for renewal of the Irish Church, no handbook, no official guide, no expert, not even a Roman document which gives all the answers. And how thankful we should be for that, for the Church is essentially a believing, worshipping, serving community, and renewal is about tapping the resources of the people, being sensitive to their mode of expressing the faith, interpreting the manifestations of the Holy Spirit. The presence of the Holy Spirit is not always immediately obvious. It may be in Gerry, careless as to sacramental life, but scrupulous in observing Lent as a time of self-denial; it may be in Micheál and Maeve who, accidentally coming upon a group of foreign visitors, took them to their home and "free-gratis-and-for-nothing" treated the strangers to an afternoon of music, song, dance and refreshment before putting them on the train for the next leg of their tour; or it may be in the vigils of the praying multitudes round Mary's shrine in the wind-swept village of Knock in Co. Mayo, or maybe in the heart of a Dublin slum where Christy, touched by the cross of Christ, could tell so vividly of the walk to Calvary in his "Good Friday". Truly, there is a "list of doors that truth had left unlatched", opportunities beyond counting for those who keep faith with the past and face tomorrow with open minds and hearts.

Good Friday

In and out among the narrow little ways of the town
    They dragged Him, bearded Man, and the
        gems of sweat
On His brow glittered like gold-dust
    In the merciless fire of noon-day.
Sticks flashed and thudded dully on straining flesh;
    Taunts, maledictions, words sharp
        with scorn and hate.
Sank as fire into the tired brain;
    Spits bright with foulness ran as lava
        down His chest,
And the cruel, thin stones of the hillside
    Made the blood run from the stumbling Feet,
Staining the earth with a crimson glory.

On they dragged Him, the cross's shadow on His back,
Up the awaiting hill, as an animal to the slaughter-house.
   He gazed forlorn, with timeless pity
      upon the deriding multitude,

Sunk in the agony of betrayal, His denied majesty
   A crown of thorns girding the tranquil brow;
And there, Fatherless, they nailed Him to a
   beam of mountain wood,

And the pain-bright eyes gazed into the deeps
     of all that had been
       and was yet to be,

Surveying His world, His desecrated Garden, hanging
      from the cross
Upon a brooding hill, a bleeding Ecstasy.[20]

Notes

CHAPTER ONE

1. *Intercom*, Vol. 6, 1975, pp. 2-5, *passim*
2. *Furrow*, Vol. 25, 1974, p. 185
3. *ibid.*
4. *ibid.*, p. 186
5. *ibid.*, p. 188
6. *Kavanagh*, "The Great Hunger", part III, p. 38
7. *ibid.*, "Memory of Brother Michael", p. 84
8. *The Irish Countryman*, p. 181
9. *Kavanagh*, "In Memory of My Mother", p. 163
10. A favourite saying of an old Co. Cork schoolmaster.
11. *Poems from the Irish*, p. 17

CHAPTER TWO

1. "Confessio", *passim*
2. *Evangelii Nutiandi*
3. "Confessio", p. 12
4. "Prehistoric Ireland", G. F. Mitchell, in *CIH*, pp. 30-33, *passim*
5. *Celtic Mythology*, p. 12
6. "The Celts", T.D. McGee, in *The Minstrel of Erin*, pp. 81-82
7. *Celtic Mythology*, p. 11
8. *ibid.*, pp. 12, 14
9. *Bards of Gael & Gall*, Preface to second ed., p. 1
10. *A Handbook of Irish Folklore*, p. iii
11. "The Beginnings of Christianity", T. Ó Fiaich, in *CIH*, p. 62
12. "Poetry of the Celtic Races and Other Stories", Ernest Renan, quoted in *Carmina Gadelica*, (i), p. xxxiii
13. *Carmina Gadelica*, (i), p. xxxiii
14. Two personal documents survive, viz. the "Confessio", and the "Letter to Coroticus", cf. *Classicalia et Mediaevalia* and *Libri Epistolarum Sancti Patricii Episcopi*, Dublin, 1952.

   A third document attributed to Patrick "The Breastplate (alias "Lorica") Faed Fiada" (Deer's Cry) is still a matter of controversy. Of it Healy says: "We have not the same certainty of the authenticity of this poem as we have of the Confession and of the Epistle to Coroticus. Very high authorities, however, declare that it is the genuine work of

our Saint, and, certainly, neither in language or sentiment is
it unworthy of him, or inconsistent with the date to which
it is ascribed" (*The Life and Writings of St. Patrick*, Dr Healy,
Dublin, 1905, pp. 560-561).

15. "Confessio", p. 18
16. *ibid.*, pp. 23-25, *passim*
17. *ibid.*, pp. 33-44
18. "The Beginnings of Christianity", (cf. 11 *supra*), p. 65
19. *ibid.*, p. 68
20. *ibid.*, p. 67
21. *Ir. Mon.*, p. 142
22. *ibid.*, pp. 144-145
23. "Early Irish Society", F. J. Byrne, in *CIH*, p. 45
24. *Manners & Customs*, (i), p. 1xxix
25. *Early Irish Literature*, p. xii
26. *The Brehon Laws*, p. 3
27. *ibid.*, pp. 5-6
28. *Manners & Customs*, (ii), p. 73
29. *ibid.*, p. 74
30. *Larousse Encyclopedia of Mythology*
31. *The Irish Tradition*, p. 46
32. *ibid.*, pp. 46-47
33. *Early Irish Society*, p. 87
34. *Pathways in Spirituality*, p. 123
35. *Manners & Customs*, (ii), p. 75
36. *The Massbook for Ireland*, p. 67. For full original text see Healy,
    (cf. 14 *supra*), pp. 705-708
37. *Pathways in Spirituality*, p. 123
38. *A Drinking Cup*, p. 17
39. *Ériu*, (i), p. 40
40. *The Irish Tradition*, p. 60
41. *Thes. Pal.*, (ii), p. 327
42. *Seven Centuries of Irish Learning*, p. 30
43. *Early Irish Poetry*, p. 14
44. "Old Ireland and her Spirituality", D. Ó Laoghaire, S.J., in *Old
    Ireland*, p. 37
45. *ITS*, (47), p. 3
46. *ibid.*, pp. 3-25, *passim*
47. *ibid.*, p. 37
48. *ibid.*
49. *ibid.*, p. 45
50. *ibid.*, p. 47
51. *ibid.*, p. 49
52. *Early Irish Lyrics*, p. 33
53. *ibid.*, p. 35
54. *Ériu*, (vi), p. 112
55. "Old Ireland and her Spirituality", (cf. 44 *supra*)
56. "Irish Spirituality in Antiquity", F. Cayré, (quoting Gougaud) in
    The Miracle of Ireland, p. 110

57. *A Drinking Cup*, p. 21
58. *Manners & Customs*, (ii), pp. 69-70
59. *A Drinking Cup*, p. 19
60. "Old Ireland and her Spirituality", (cf. 44 *supra*), p. 41
61. *ibid.*, p. 47
62. "Confessio", pp. 30-31
63. "The Beginnings of Christianity", (cf. 11 *supra*), p. 68
64. *Sancti Columbani Opera*, p. 122
65. *Ir. Mon.*, p. 335
66, *Ireland of the Saints*, p. 106
67. *The Irish Tradition*, p. 53
68. *A Drinking Cup*, p. 15
69. *Early Irish Lyrics*, pp. 41-43
70. *Ir. Mon.*, p. 349
71. *Manners & Customs*, (ii), p. 74
72. *Féilire*, p. xlix
73. *Ir. Mon.* p. 348
74. *Féilire*, p. xlix
75. *Féilire, passim*
76. *Ir. Mon.*, pp. 391-392
77. *Lismore*, p. 259
78. *Early Irish Literature*, p. 80
79. *The Book of Irish Curses*, p. 39
80. *Féilire*, p. 56; *The Irish Tradition*, p. 62
81. The manuscript known as "The Book of Kells" is preserved in Trinity College, Dublin.
82. The chalice, unearthed in a fort at Ardagh, Co. Limerick — hence its name — is in the National Museum, Dublin.
83. *The Irish Story*, pp. 34-35
84. *ibid.*, p. 35
85. *Ireland of the Saints*, p. 69
86. cf. stanza 3, line 3 of Rolleston's poem, 87 *inf.*
87. *A Book of Ireland*, p. 50
88. *The Early Monastic Schools of Ireland*, p. 2
89. *McManus*, p. 216
90. *Monks of the West from St. Benedict to St. Bernard*, pp. 298-299
91. *McManus*, pp. 217-218
92. *The Irish*, p. 50
93. *The Irish Story*, p. 26
94. *McManus*, p. 215
95. *Sancti Columbani Opera*, pp. 46-49
96. *Ériu*, (v), pp. 110-111
97. *Studies*, No. 65, p. 39
98. *Lismore*, pp. 169-170
99. *Studies*, No. 65, p. 41
100. *The Irish Tradition*, p. 39
101. *ibid.*, p. 39
102. *ibid.*, p. 58
103. *Studies*, No. 66, p. 230

104. *Studies*, No. 65, p. 47
105. *ibid.*
106. *Studies*, No. 66, p. 235
107. *ibid.*, p. 236
108. *ibid.*, p. 242
109. *McManus*, pp. 212-213
110. *Celtic Mythology*, p. 131-132
111. *Bards of Gael & Gall*, pp. 207-208; *Early Irish Lyrics*, p. 52

CHAPTER THREE

1. *Féilire*, p. 210; *Thes. Pal.*, (ii), p. 306
2. *Early Irish Lyrics*, p. 71
3. *Seven Centuries of Irish Learning*, *passim*
4. *Annals of Loch Cé*
5. *IER*, Vol. 71, 1949, p. 142
6. *ibid.*, p. 143
7. *ibid.*
8. *Seven Centuries of Irish Learning*, pp. 14-15
9. *ibid.*, p. 15
10. *Calendar of Ormond Deeds*, (ii), pp. 168-169
11. *ibid.*, p. 169
12. *The Irish Tradition*, p. 115
13. *Life of Patrick*, pp. 661-662
14. *ibid.*, p. 659
15. *ibid.*, p. 664
16. *ibid.*, p. 658
17. *ITS*, Vol. 23, p. 290
18. *ibid.*, pp. 291-292
19. *Early Irish Literature*, p. 101
20. *ibid.*, p. 37
21. *Irish Classical Poetry*, p. 77
22. *ibid.*, pp. 77-78
23. *HIC*, (ii), fasc. 5, p. 42
24. *Dánta Dé*, p. 49 also *HIC*, (ii), fasc. 5, p. 33, footnote
25. *Irish Bardic Poetry*, p. 302
26. *Dánta Aonghus Fionn O Dálaigh*, pp. viii – xiii, *passim*
27. *Irish Bardic Poetry*, p. 302
28. *ibid.*, p. 301-302
29. *ITS*, Vol. 22, p. 219 (English translation: *ITS*, Vol. 23, p. 145)
30. *ibid.*, Vol. 22, p. 242 (Englis translation: *ITS*, Vol. 23, p. 159)
31. *The Integral Irish Tradition*, pp. 11-12
32. *ibid.*, p. 9
33. *ibid.*
34. *Irish Spirituality*, p. 5
35. *ibid.*, p. 12
36. *ibid.*

37. *HIC*, (ii), fasc. 5, "The Church in Gaelic Ireland: 13th-15th centuries", Canice Mooney, O.F.M., p. 56
38. *ibid.*
39. *ibid.*
40. *ibid.*, p. 59
41. *HIC*, (ii), fasc. 5, p. 57
42. IER, Vol. 99, 1963, p. 106
43. HIC, (ii), fasc. 5, p. 18
44. *ibid.*
45. *ibid.*
46. *ibid.*, p. 20
47. *ibid.*, p. 61
48. *Irish Spirituality*, pp. 8-9
49. *ibid.*, p. 10
50. *IER*, Vol. 99, 1963, pp. 104-105
51. *ibid.*, p. 102
52. *A Book of Ireland*, pp. 82-84

CHAPTER FOUR

1. *IER*, Vo. 99, 1963, p. 107
2. This phrase is common in the ancient Annals, e.g. *Annals of Loch Cé* under the year A.D. 1118: 'Diarmaid Ua Briain, king of Mumha, and of all Leth-Mogha, died at Corcachmor of Mumha, after unction and penance."
3. *IER*, Vol. 99, 1963, p. 103
4. *IER*, Vol. 69, 1947, p. 136
5. *History of Ireland*, (ii), p. 210-211
6. *ibid.*, p. 212
7. "The Tudor Conquest", G. A. Hayes-McCoy, in *CIH*, p. 181
8. *Lecky*, quoted by McLysaght, p. 281
9. *McLysaght*, p. 284
10. "The Tudor Conquest", (cf. 7 *supra*). p. 181
11. *ibid.*, p. 180, quoting from a statement of Thomas Lynch of Galway (State papers, Henry VIII, Ireland, iii, p. 141)
12. *McLysaght*, pp. 281-282
13. *ibid.*, p. 282 and cf. footnote
14. "Survival and Reorganisation, 1650-95", B. Millett, O.F.M., in *CIH*, (iii), fasc. 8, p. 2
15. *ibid.*
16. *ibid.*, p. 57, quoting from Carlyle's *Cromwell's Letters and Speeches*, (ii), London, 1846, p. 86
17. *Cambrensis Eversus*, Gratianus Lucius, Hibernus (1662), Dublin, 1848, pp. 72-73, footnote "h"
18. "The Tudor Conquest, (cf. 7 *supra*), p. 181
19. "The Church Under the Penal Code", J. Brady and P. J. Corish, in *HIC*, (iv), fasc. 2, p. 5

20. "The Origins of Catholic Nationalism", P. J. Corish, in *Hic*, (iii), fasc. 8, p. 57
21. *Young's Tour*, (ii), part 2, p. 44, also "The Church under the Penal Code", (cf. 19 *supra*), p. 22
22. *The Hidden Ireland*
23. "The Restoration and the Jacobite War", J. G. Simms, in *CIH*, p. 206, quoting *Poems of David Ó Bruadair*, J. C. MacErlain (ed.), (iii), 1917, p. 15
24. *Lecky*, quoted in *The Road Around Ireland*, p. 436
25. *HIC*, (v), p. 2
26. *McLysaght*, p. 278
27. "The Origins of Catholic Nationalism", P. J. Corish, in *HIC*, (iii), fasc. 8, p. 30
28. *Old Irish Links with France*, p. 19 footnote 2
29. *ibid.*, p. 19
30. *Ár bPaidreacha Dúchais*
31. *Our Mass our Life*, p. 8
32. *ibid.*
33. *ibid.*
34. *ibid.*, p. 11
35. *ibid.*, p. 12
36. *ibid.*, pp. 16-17
37. *ibid.*, p. 17 , footnote 1
38. Some of the more notable collections include:
    (i) *Ár bPaidreacha Dúchais*, (cf. 30 *supra*);
    (ii) *Paidreacha na nDaoine*, Searloid Ní Dhéisighe;
    (iii) *Prayers of the Gael*, R. MacCrocaigh, (being a translation of *Paidreacha na nDaoine*);
    (iv) *Religious Songs of Connaught*, Douglas Hyde;
    (v) *Urnaighe na nGael*, an tAthair Uinseann, O.C.S.O.;
    (vi) *Our Mass our Life*, Diarmuid Ó Laoghaire, S.J..
39. *Our Mass our Life*, p. 27
40. *ibid.*, p. 24
41. *ibid.*, pp. 28-29
42. *ibid.*, p. 36
43. *Constitutio Ecclesiasticae*, (i), pp. 132-133
44. *IER*, Vol. 70, 1948, p. 516
45. *A Bishop of the Penal Times*, p. 18
46. *ibid.*, p. 22
47. *ibid.*, p. 34
48. *Borstal Boy*, p. 330
49. *Irish Spirituality*, pp. 9-10
50. *Irish Pilgrimage*, p. 29
51. *ibid.*
52. *Constitutio Ecclesiasticae*, (ii), p. 416
53. *Prayers of the Gael*, p. 56
54. *Paidreacha na nDaoine*
55. *Prayers of the Gael*, p. 59
56. *ibid.*, p. 57

57. *Carolan – the Life, Times & Music of an Irish Harper*, (ii), p. 146
58. *Carmina Gadelica*, (i), p. xxxiii
59. *Old Irish Links with France*, p. 13

CHAPTER FIVE

1. *Fennell*, p. 1
2. *ibid.*
3. *ibid.*, p. 31
4. *IER*, Vol. 70, 1948, pp. 520-521
5. *ibid.*, p. 521
6. *ibid.*
7. *ibid.*
8. *Fennell*, p. 15
9. *ibid.*, p. 37
10. *Annals of Ulster*, 4 vols, Dublin, 1887-1901, (iii), pp. 428, 430
11. *Constitutio Ecclesiasticae*, (ii), p. 370
12. "Marriage and population growth in Ireland, 1750-1845", in *Economic History Review*, 2nd series, xvi, 1963, pp. 301-13; also *Ireland since the Famine*, F.S.L. Lyons, Glasgow, 1974, pp. 39-41 and footnotes *passim*; *MyLysaght*, chapter III, "marriage in its full sense was common at seventeen or eighteen", p. 46 and *passim*
13. *Fennell*, p. 41
14. *Furrow*, Vo. 10, 1959, p. 673
15. *De Bhál*, pp. 211-214
16. *ibid.*, p. 212
17. *ibid.*
18. *ibid.*
19. *ibid.*, p. 214
20. *Fennell*, p. 37
21, *ITQ*, Vol. 26, 1959, p. 134, quoting *The Freeman's Journal* of 23 August 1850
22. *ibid.*, p. 136
23. *AHR*, Vol. 77, 1972, p. 638
24. *Canon*, p. 127
25. *ibid.*, pp. 127-28
26. *ITQ*, Vol. 26, 1959, p. 132
27. *Paul Cullen and His Contemporaries*, (i), p. 331
28. *AHR*, Vol. 77, 1972, p. 648
29. *Allocutions to the Clergy & Pastorals of the late Right Rev. Dr. Moriarty, Bishop of Kerry*, p. 64
30. *ibid.*, p. 65
31. *AHR*, Vol. 77, 1972, p. 635
32. *ibid.*, p. 636
33. *ibid.*
34. *ITQ*, Vol. 26, 1959, p. 140 *et seq.*

35. *ibid.*, p. 141
36. *ibid.*
37. *AHR*, Vol. 77, 1972, p. 636
38. *ITQ*, Vol. 26, 1959, p. 140
39. *AHR*, Vol. 77, 1972, p. 625
40. *ibid.*, p. 637
41. *ibid.*, p. 638
42. *ibid.*
43. *ibid.*, p. 646
44. Dating roughly from Cullen's arrival in Ireland in 1850.
45. *AHR*, Vol. 77, 1972, p. 625
46. *Furrow*, Vol. 27, 1976, p. 583
47. *Poems, 1955-1966*, p. 203

CHAPTER SIX

1. *Kavanagh*, "In Memory of my Mother", p. 163
2. *Kerry Archaeological Journal*, Vol. 6, 1973, pp. 83-100
3. *ibid.*, p. 98
4. *ibid.*
5. *It all Happened*, p. 30
6. *Kerry Archaeological Journal*, Vol. 6, 1973, pp. 98-99
7. *Young's Tour*, (ii), pp. 146-47
8. *Kerry Archaeological Journal*, Vol. 6, 1973, pp. 83-100
9. *Young's Tour*, (ii), p. 147
10. *The Year in Ireland*, p. 228
11. *The Farm by Lough Gur*, Mary Carbery, Cork, 1973, p. 204
12. *Knock: The Shrine of the Pilgrim People of God*, pp. 103-104
13. "Rounds" refers to the movement "dishel", i.e. right-handedly or sun-wise around the well, or holy place; during the movement certain prayers are prescribed — usually a certain number of Paters, Aves or Glorias, or, as in Knock, the fifteen mysteries of the rosary.
14. *The Festival of Lughnasa, passim*
15. *Addict for Christ*, p. 5
16. *ibid.*, p. 8
17. *The Making of Matt Talbot*, pp. 18-27, *passim*
18. *The Correspondence of Daniel O'Connell*, (ii), p. 95
19. *ibid.*, p. 97
20. *Background Music*, p. 7

Bibliography

A Book of Ireland, F. O'Connor (ed.), London, 1971
A Calendar of Ormond Deeds, 6 vols, E. Curtis, Dublin, 1932-1971
Addict for Christ, F. Johnston, Dublin, no date
A Drinking Cup, B. Kenneally, Dublin, 1970
A Handbook of Irish Folklore, S. Ó Súilleabháin, Dublin, 1942
A History of Ireland in the Eighteenth Century, 5 vols, W. Lecky, London, 1892
A History of Irish Catholicism, 6 vols, P. J. Corish (ed.), Dublin, 1967-1970
Allocutions to the Clergy and Pastorals of the late Right Rev. Dr. Moriarty, Bishop of Kerry, Dr Moriarty, Dublin 1884
Annala Uladh — Annals of Ulster, 4 vols, B. MacCarthy (ed.), Dublin, 1887-1901
Annals of Loch Cé, W. M. Hennessy (ed.), London, 1871
Ár bPaidreacha Dúchais, D. Ó Laoghaire, Dublin, 1975
Arthur Young's Tour in Ireland, 2 vols, A. W. Hutton (ed), London, 1892

Background Music, C. Brown, London, 1973
Bards of the Gael and Gall, G. Sigerson, Dublin, 1907
Borstal Boy, B. Behan, London, 1975

Cambrensis Eversus, 3 vols, G. Lucius, Dublin, 1848
Carmina Gadelica, 6 vols, A. Carmichael, Edinburgh, 1928
Carolan — the Life, Times and Music of an Irish Harper, 2 vols, D. O'Sullivan, London, 1958
Celtic Mythology, P. MacCanna, New York, 1973
Collected Poems, P. Kavanagh, London, 1972

Dánta Dé, L. McKenna (ed.), Dublin, 1922
Dánta Aonghus Fionn Ó Dalaigh, L. McKenna (ed.), Dublin & London, 1919
Discovering Kerry, T. J. Barrington, Dublin, 1976

Early Irish Literature, G. Murphy and E. Knott, London, 1967
Early Irish Literature, M. Dillon, Chicago & London, 1948
Early Irish Lyrics, G. Murphy, Oxford, 1956
Early Irish Poetry, J. Carney, Cork, 1969
Early Irish Society, M. Dillon, Cork, 1969
Evangelii Nuntiandi, Pope Paul VI, London, no date

Féilire Oengusso Ceili Dé – The Martyrology of Oengus the Culdee, W. Strokes (ed.), London, 1905

History of Ireland, S. O'Halloran, New York, no date, probably c. 1850

Ireland of the Saints, D. D. C. Pochin Mould, London, 1953
Irish Bardic Poetry, O. J. Bergin, Dublin, 1970
Irish Classical Poetry, E. Knott, Cork, 1973
Irish Life in the Seventeenth Century, E. MyLysaght, Dublin, 1939
Irish Monasticism, J. Ryan, Dublin, 1931
Irish Pilgrimage, D. D. C. Pochin Mould, Dublin, 1955
It All Happened, S. Fenton, Dublin, 1949

Knock: The Shrine of the Pilgrim People of God, M. Walsh, Tuam, 1967

Larousse Encyclopedia of Mythology, Hamlyn, London, 1965
Lives of Saints from The Book of Lismore, W. Stokes (ed.), Oxford, 1890

Manners and Customs of the Ancient Irish, 3 vols, E. O'Curry, London, 1873
Medieval Irish Lyrics, J. Carney, Dublin, 1967

Old Ireland, R. McNally (ed.), Dublin, 1965
Old Irish links with France, R. Hayes, Dublin, 1940
Our Mass our Life, D. Ó Laoghaire, Dublin, no date

Paidreacha na nDaoine, S. Ní Dheisighe, Dublin, 1924
Pathways in Spirituality, J. Macquarrie, Bristol, 1972

Patrick in his own words, J. Duffy, Veritas, Dublin, 1975
Paul Cullen and His Contemporaries, 4 vols, P. Mac Suibhne, Naas, 1962
Poems 1955-1966, A. Clarke, Dublin, 1974
Poems from the Irish, Douglas Hyde, Dublin, 1963
Prayers of the Gael, R. MacCrócaigh, Edinburgh, 1914

Sancti Columbani Opera, G. S. M. Walker (ed.), Dublin, 1957
Seven Centuries of Irish Learning, B. Ó Cuív (ed.), Cork, 1971

The Book of Irish Curses, P. Power, Cork, 1974
The Brehon Laws, Ginnell, London, 1894
The Changing Face of Catholic Ireland, D. Fennell (ed.), Dublin, 1968
The Correspondence of Daniel O'Connell, 2 vols, M. R. O'Connell,
                    Shannon, 1972
The Course of Irish History, T. W. Moody and F. X. Martin (eds), Cork,
                    1967
The Early Monastic Schools of Ireland, W. G. Hanson, Cambridge, 1927
The Festival of Lughnasa, M. McNeill, Oxford, 1962
The Hidden Ireland, D. Corkery, Dublin, 1925
The Irish, S. Ó Faolain, Hammondsworth, 1969
The Irish Countryman, C. Arensberg, Glouster, Mass., 1959
The Irish Story, A. Curtayne, Dublin, 1962
The Irish Tradtion, R. Flower, Oxford, 1947
The Life and Writings of St. Patrick, J. Healy, Dublin, 1905
The Making of Matt Talbot, M. Purcell, Dublin 1972
The Massbook for Ireland, N. Watson (ed.), Dublin, 1969
The Minstrel of Erin, T. O'Hanlon, Dublin, 1930
The Miracle of Ireland, H. Daniel-Rops, Dublin & London, 1959
The Monks of the West from St. Benedict to St. Bernard, 7 vols, Count
                    de Montalembert, Edinburgh & London, 1861-1879
The Road Round Ireland, P. Colum, New York, 1927
Thesaurus Palaeohibernicus, 2 vols, W. Stokes and J. Strachan (eds),
                    Cambridge, 1901-1903
The Story of the Irish Race, S. McManus, New York, 1969
The Year in Ireland, K. Danaher, Cork, 1973